TRADE PROMOTION COORDINATING COMMITTEE

2008 National Export Strategy

THE NEW GLOBAL MAIN STREET

UNITED STATES OF AMERICA

CONTENTS

APPENDICES

Dear Mr. President and Madam Speaker:

On behalf of the Administration and as Chairman of the Trade Promotion Coordinating Committee (TPCC), it is my pleasure to present the *2008 National Export Strategy.*

The United States remains the world's largest exporter, and U.S. exports are growing sharply. In 2007, U.S. goods and services exports grew by 13 percent, to a record $1.6 trillion. In 2007, exports accounted for 41 percent of growth in the U.S. economy. In the first quarter of 2008, exports comprised 12.6 percent of the U.S. gross domestic product, compared to 9.5 percent five years ago. Foreign demand for U.S. goods is bolstering the balance sheets of major U.S. corporations. Overseas sales are keeping the factory floors of small businesses humming. The influx of foreign tourists is providing revenue to local communities.

Exporting is part of our daily lives. Exports benefit American families, communities, and towns, and help to make our economy the strongest and most competitive in the world.

As outlined in the chapter **State of Trade,** we are experiencing a historic set of favorable conditions for U.S. exports. Rising foreign incomes represent strong foreign demand. Changes in exchange rates make American goods more price-competitive in many markets. And foreign tariffs and communications costs have fallen.

Thousands of U.S. companies are not aware of export opportunities or the programs available to help them. The challenge is reaching these companies amidst a U.S. business community of 27 million firms. The centerpiece of our National Export Strategy, as presented in the chapter **Broadening and Deepening the Base of Exporters,** is to engage in partnerships with other service providers to reach more potential exporters. We will strengthen partnerships with American cities and States, with large service corporations that have millions of daily contacts with clients, and with trade associations and other nonprofit organizations that have unique access to potential exporters.

As a Nation, we also must recognize that our economic well-being is rooted in our openness to the rest of the world. Openness plays to the strengths of American industry—its innovation and productivity. It improves consumer choice and living standards at home, while giving our firms the opportunity to compete for business abroad. The United States has led the world in creating a more open trading environment by breaking down foreign barriers to trade and continues to work toward a successful conclusion of the Doha Development Round of World Trade Organization (WTO) multilateral trade negotiations. As highlighted in the chapter **Free Trade Agreements,** we have expanded opportunity for U.S. exporters through bilateral and regional Free Trade Agreements (FTAs). In 2007, exports to our 14 FTA trade partner countries accounted for one-quarter of the growth since 2006 of U.S. exports of goods. TPCC agencies will continue to promote the benefits of these agreements and create opportunities for U.S. companies to enter these markets.

Millions of people have been lifted out of poverty through participation in the global trading system, at the same time creating vast new markets for American exports. In the chapter **Priority Markets,** we look at China, India, Brazil, and Russia. In 2007, U.S. exports set impressive records in all four countries. The National Export Strategy targets these economies based on their commercial potential as well as the difficulties U.S. companies experience in entering these markets.

In the chapter **Next Generation Markets,** we focus on the Middle East and Africa, two regions that continue to experience rapid economic growth. In these two regions, we see enormous spending on infrastructure projects, as well as new import demand driven by reforms and expanded credit. In sub-Saharan Africa, many markets are benefiting from global demand for commodities and bearing the fruits of years of structural reforms. Together, the TPCC agencies are focusing on helping U.S. exporters navigate these markets while mitigating their risks.

I commend the other TPCC agencies in their efforts with the Department of Commerce to ensure that the U.S. Government has the right programs in the right markets to help U.S. companies export. We will broaden the base of exporters through strategic partnerships. We will introduce more companies to FTA markets. We will ensure that exporters large and small have the tools to conquer the uncertainties of doing business in priority emerging markets. And we will advance our commercial relationships with the next generation of emerging markets.

America has maintained its innovative edge in the world and is creating a culture of exporting. Now is the time to build on our success and continue opening new markets, recognizing openness as our strength.

Sincerely,

Carlos M. Gutierrez
Secretary of Commerce and
Chairman of the Trade Promotion
Coordinating Committee

State of Trade

U.S. exporters are hitting their stride in the global economy, with record exports making an increasingly important contribution to overall U.S. economic growth. The prospects for U.S. exports are better than any time in recent memory across sectors and for U.S. companies large and small, due to the rapid growth of foreign markets and favorable terms of trade. The services sector continues to make an outsized contribution to growth in exports and improvements in the trade balance. And for smaller firms in particular, e-commerce continues to shrink distances and transaction costs between buyers and sellers.

American firms are maintaining their innovative and competitive edge in the world while developing their own new culture of exporting. In the process, they are discovering that in addition to their local Main Street USA, they now have access to the new global Main Street.

OVERVIEW OF U.S. TRADE

Record Exports: In 2007, U.S. goods and services exports grew by 13 percent, reaching an all-time high of $1.646 trillion, including record goods exports of $1.148 trillion (including

CHART 1
EXPORTS BY MAJOR SECTOR

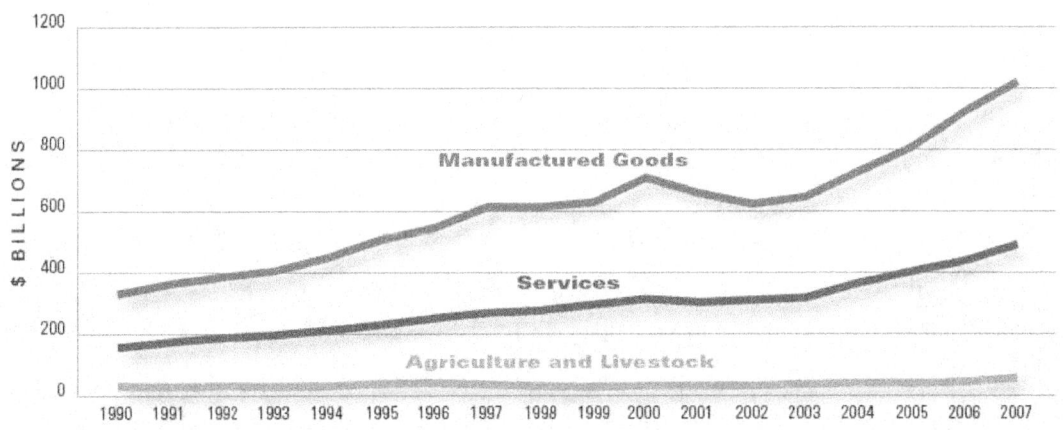

Notes: Manufactured Goods total includes North American Industry Classification System (NAICS) categories 31, 32, and 33. Agriculture & Livestock includes products in NAICS 11. Services Trade is calculated on a Balance of Payments basis. Sectors cannot be added to arrive at a trade total.

Source: U.S. Department of Commerce, International Trade Administration, TradeStats Express™

record agricultural exports) and record services exports of $497 billion.[1] U.S. exports grew solidly in all sectors—manufacturing, services, and agriculture *(Chart 1)*.

In 2007, goods exports increased by $126 billion over 2006, with records in agricultural domestic exports ($89.9 billion); industrial supplies and materials ($316.3 billion); capital goods ($447.4 billion); consumer goods ($146.1 billion); and automotive vehicles, parts, and engines ($121.0 billion). U.S. exports to our major trading partners also set records: Canada ($248.9 billion); Mexico ($136.1 billion); the European Union ($247.2 billion); China ($65.2 billion); and South/Central America and the Caribbean ($107.5 billion). The United States also set records in exports to other key emerging markets, including a 28 percent increase in exports to Brazil (to $24.6 billion); a 57 percent increase in exports to Russia (to $7.4 billion); and a 75 percent increase in exports to India (to $17.6 billion).

Agricultural trade continues to show a surplus as agricultural domestic exports set a record of $89.9 billion in 2007, contributing $17.9 billion to the balance of payments—a trend that has continued since 1959. More than 1 million jobs, both on and off the farm, are supported by agricultural exports.

THE RETURN OF TRAVEL AND TOURISM

International visitors spent a record $122 billion in 2007 in the United States, a 13 percent increase over 2006. This spending represents a second straight year of record tourism exports* and a 53 percent increase over the lows following September 11, 2001. The number of visitors also set records, growing 10 percent to 56 million travelers to the United States. Ten of the top 25 markets broke records, with North American Free Trade Agreement (NAFTA) trading partners Canada and Mexico accounting for well over half of all international visitors. Top overseas countries included the United Kingdom, Japan, Germany, France, and South Korea. Some of the steepest increases in visitors came from Asia (India, China) and South America (Brazil, Venezuela, Colombia, and Argentina). The U.S. travel and tourism industry is valued at $1.3 trillion, employs 8.7 million people, and has generated trade surpluses for 19 consecutive years. Travel and tourism account for 8 percent of all U.S. exports and 25 percent of services sector exports.

* Spending by international travelers while in the United States, including passenger fares, is defined as a U.S. export.

Services exports increased by $63 billion in 2007. Increases occurred in private services ($34.4 billion), which include business, professional, technical, insurance, and financial services; travel ($11.0 billion); royalties and license fees ($10.4 billion); other transportation ($5.3 billion), which includes freight and port services; and passenger fares ($3.6 billion).

Export growth in all sectors has kept the United States the world's top exporter of goods and services, ahead of Germany, China, and Japan *(Chart 2)*.

1   U.S. Department of Commerce, Bureau of the Census, FT900: U.S. International Trade in Goods and Services April 2008 (June 10, 2008), 4.

CHART 2
TOP TEN EXPORTERS: GOODS AND SERVICES, 2007

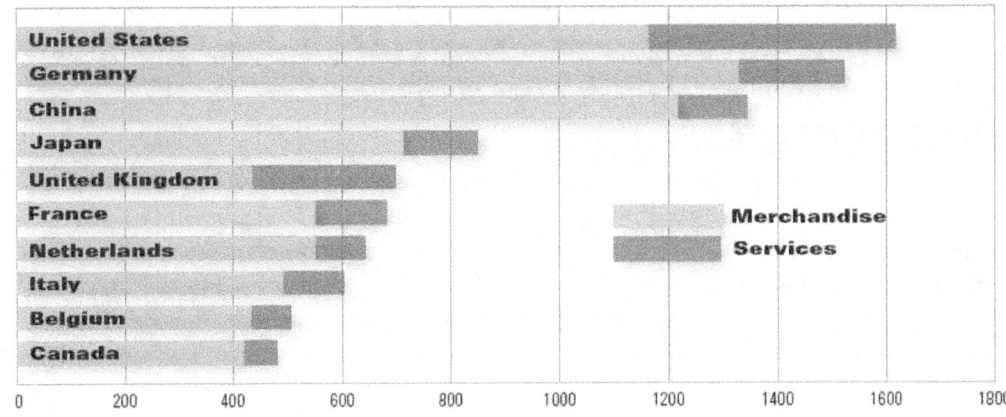

$ BILLIONS

Source: World Trade Organization,
"World Trade 2007, Prospects for
2008," Tables 3 and 5.

CHART 3
TRADE AS PERCENTAGE OF U.S. ECONOMY

PERCENT OF GROSS DOMESTIC PRODUCT

*Note: Trade figures are for
the export and import of
goods and services.*

Source: U.S. Department of Commerce,
Bureau of Economic Analysis, *National
Income and Product Accounts,* Table
1.1.10. Percentage Shares of Gross
Domestic Product, last revised March
27, 2008.

Impact of Exports on the Economy: Strong U.S. exports are playing an important role in supporting the U.S. economy during the current period of economic adjustment. As noted in the Council of Economic Advisers' *Economic Report of the President,* "The rapid growth of U.S. exports has been one of the most important economic developments of the past few years."[2] After four straight years of double-digit growth, exports in 2007 account for a growing share of the U.S. economy *(Chart 3).* Between 2003 and 2007, real exports grew 37.4 percent while real Gross Domestic Product (GDP) grew only 12.3 percent. A faster-growing export sector increased its share of nominal GDP to a record 11.9 percent in 2007.[3] In 2007, exports accounted for 41.4 percent of the growth of the U.S. economy in terms of the change in real GDP.[4]

Imports and the Trade Balance: Exports are also growing faster than imports. Although U.S. imports also reached record levels in 2007, imports grew at a much slower rate, and as a

2   Council of Economic Advisers, *Economic Report of the President, 2008* (Washington, D.C.: Government Printing Office, 2008) 79.
3   U.S. Department of Commerce, Bureau of Economic Analysis, "Gross Domestic Product: Fourth Quarter 2007," news release, March 27, 2008, Table 3.
4   Ibid., Table 2.

EXPORT SUCCESS
FARIBAULT WOOLEN MILLS, Faribault, Minnesota

"We have been greatly rewarded as international sales have continued to bolster our company's growth, and exporting has allowed us to sustain jobs locally."
—Michael Harris, President and CEO

Faribault sells to more than 20 countries, with the Nordic markets—Norway, Denmark, Sweden, Finland, and Iceland—being one of its most important export regions. The Department of Commerce encouraged Faribault to exhibit at Heimtextil 2006. Held annually in Frankfurt, Germany, Heimtextil is one of Europe's premier textile and apparel trade shows. In addition to guidance on branding and direct promotional activities, Department of Commerce offices throughout the Nordic region recruited foreign buyers to attend Heimtextil. As a result, Faribault met and signed up several distributors now selling Faribault's line of woolen products in Europe.

result, the overall trade balance improved for the first time since 2001. In 2007, the annual increase in the value of exports ($188.7 billion) overtook the annual increase in the value of imports ($135.7 billion), reducing the overall trade deficit by $53.0 billion to $700.3 billion. As a percentage of GDP, the goods and services deficit was 5.1 percent in 2007, down from 5.8 percent in 2006. The services sector played a major role, showing an impressive $119.1 billion trade surplus to offset some of the $819.4 billion deficit in goods (on a balance of payments basis). While the bilateral deficit with China grew in 2007, the annual deficits with Canada and the European Union decreased.

Petroleum's Growing Share of Imports and the Trade Deficit: With prices for a barrel of oil continuing to rise, petroleum has become a more significant factor in the overall trade balance *(Chart 4)*. In 2007, the average price per barrel of imported crude oil was $64.28,

CHART 4
IMPACT OF PETROLEUM IMPORTS, 1983–2007

Note: Dollar figures are actual unrevised dollars. Petroleum products consist of all products classified under Standard International Trade Classification (SITC) Rev. 3 code 33.

Source: U.S. Department of Commerce, Bureau of the Census, Foreign Trade Division.

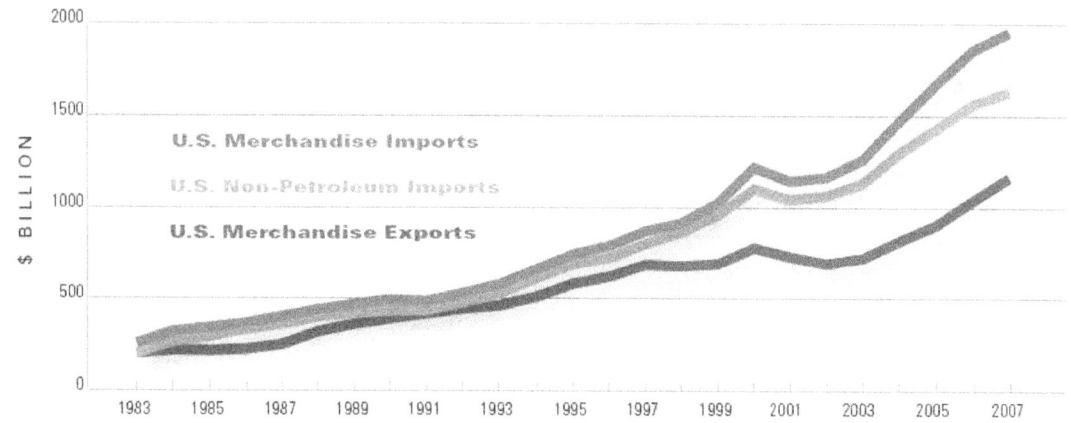

resulting in a record petroleum deficit of $293.2 billion,[5] or 36 percent of the merchandise trade deficit. In the first four months of 2008 (January to April), the average price of imported oil rose to a record $88.84, resulting in a petroleum deficit of $132.1 billion, or 48 percent of the merchandise trade deficit. With the price of imported oil rising to $96.81 in April 2008 (latest data available), petroleum's share of imports and the trade deficit continues to grow. [6]

FACTORS CONTRIBUTING TO U.S. EXPORT GROWTH

The 2008 *Economic Report of the President*[7] points to four factors contributing to strong U.S. export performance:

1. *Foreign Income Growth:* Recent years have experienced a period of strong worldwide growth led by fast-growing emerging markets such as China, relatively strong growth in Europe, and robust GDP growth in Latin America. Most U.S. exports of goods are capital goods, consumer durable goods, and inputs that are used to produce them, and are therefore very sensitive to changes in foreign GDP.

2. *Growth in Domestic Production:* As the U.S. economy's productive capacity expands, its ability to produce goods and services for exports likely expands as well. A key factor in increasing U.S. production has been the growth of labor productivity. Gross output produced per hour of work increased in 88 percent of manufacturing industries from 2004 to 2005 (most recent data).

3. *Exchange Rates:* From January 2002 through December 2007, the dollar depreciated 23 percent in nominal terms against a weighted average of currencies. Changes in the terms of trade associated with recent exchange rate trends made U.S. goods cheaper relative to those of some other countries.

4. *Trade Costs and Barriers:* Falling costs are supporting the growth of trade, including improved communications (e.g., e-commerce and the Internet). Trade liberalization has also been important, including the reduction of trade barriers through regional and bilateral free trade agreements (FTAs). In 2007, the United States exported goods to more than 200 economies. Exports to our 14 FTA partners with agreements in force that year accounted for nearly one-quarter of the growth of U.S. goods exports between 2006 and 2007.

Resilient Global Economy and Expanding World Trade: Although economic growth in both advanced and developing economies has slowed this year, growth in emerging and developing economies is expected to continue at an impressive rate. According to the International Monetary Fund's (IMF) *World Economic Outlook*,[8] the ongoing financial crisis is forecast to slow world growth from 5.0 percent in 2007 to 4.1 percent in 2008 *(Chart 5).* Economic growth in the advanced economies is forecast to slow from 2.7 percent to 1.7 percent growth. Rapidly globalizing emerging economies have been less affected by financial market tur-

5 U.S. Department of Commerce, Bureau of the Census, *FT900: U.S. International Trade in Goods and Services April 2008* (June 10, 2008), 14.

6 Ibid., 25.

7 Council of Economic Advisers, "The Causes and Consequences of Export Growth," *Economic Report of the President* (Washington, D.C.: U.S. Government Printing Office, 2008), 79-95.

8 International Monetary Fund, *World Economic Outlook Update*, July 2008, www.imf.org/external/pubs/ft/weo/2008/update/02/index.htm.

CHART 5
WORLD OUTPUT (ANNUAL PERCENT CHANGE)

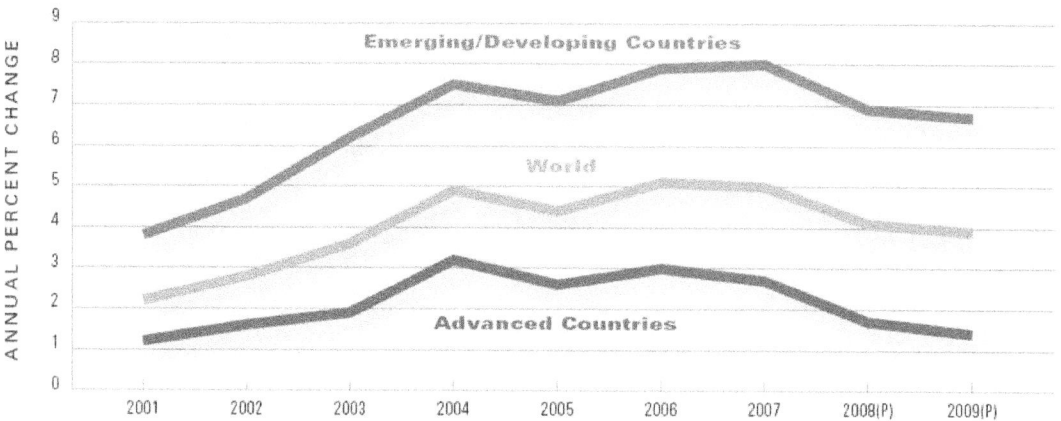

Note: 2008 and 2009 are projections.

Source : IMF, *World Economic Outlook*, July 2008, Table 1 "World Economic Outlook Update Projections," p. 4.

bulence than the advanced economies. Growth in the emerging and developing countries is moderating, but is expected to still achieve an impressive 6.9 percent growth rate. This growth rate is driven primarily by India and China, but also includes solid growth in Africa and Latin America.

As a result, the emerging and developing economies are now playing an important role in helping to undergird the world economy at a time of economic uncertainty. The IMF credits strong growth in emerging and developing countries to global integration of these economies, commodities prices, and stronger institutions and macroeconomic policy frameworks.[9] Together, these factors have led to the strongest and broadest run of global growth since the 1960s.

The expansion of world trade has been even more impressive. According to the World Bank, world trade volumes have increased at an average rate of 6.7 percent over the past seven years.[10] On the export side, the exports of developing countries (10.8 percent) have grown twice as fast as those of high-income countries (5.1 percent) since 2000. More impressive is the growth of imports in developing countries, which—boosted by these countries' new spending power—grew 14.3 percent in 2006 compared with 7.9 percent in high-income countries.[11] As a result, developing countries continue to account for a growing share of world imports. Since 1988, the industrial countries' share of global imports (excluding the United States) has declined by 13 percent, from 65 percent in 1988 to 52 percent in 2007 *(Chart 6)*, according to IMF data. Conversely, the emerging and developing countries' share of imports has grown 13 percent over this same period to 48 percent in 2007.

E-Commerce's Growing Role in Global Trade: Another major trend driving trade is the explosive growth of the Internet and e-commerce. There are 1.4 billion Internet users in the world today, according to March 2008 data from Internetworldstats.com. With 237 million users, the United States still has more Internet users than any other country, followed by

9 Subir Lall, "IMF Predicts Slower World Growth Amid Serious Market Crisis," *IMF Survey Magazine* (April 9, 2008), www.imf.org/external/pubs/ft/survey/so/2008/RES040908A.htm.

10 World Bank, *Global Economic Prospects: 2008*, 33, http://siteresources.worldbank.org/INTGEP2008/Resources/complete-report.pdf.

11 World Bank, "Rapid Growth in Developing Country Trade," *Global Economic Prospects 2008: Technological Diffusion in the Developing World* (Washington, D.C.: World Bank) 33.

CHART 6

**SHARE OF WORLD IMPORTS (EXCLUDING U.S. IMPORTS)
INDUSTRIAL VS. EMERGING AND DEVELOPING COUNTRIES, 1988–2007**

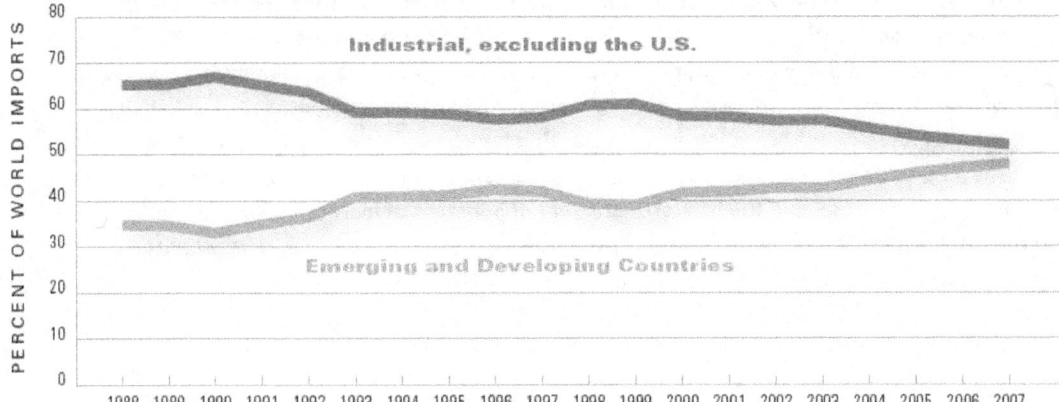

Source: IMF, International Financial Statistics (IFS). Based on data downloaded from Global Insight Database on May 12, 2008.

China (210 million), Japan (87 million), India (60 million), Germany (53 million), and Brazil (43 million). But with U.S. Internet penetration more than 71 percent, and new user growth much higher in other regions, Internet use in other countries is becoming more important for future growth. Asia now accounts for 38 percent of all Internet users, followed by Europe (27 percent), North America (18 percent), and Latin America and the Caribbean (10 percent). While Africa and the Middle East represent much smaller shares, these two regions represent by far the fastest growth of Internet users since 2000.

At the same time, the link between the Internet and e-commerce grows stronger, shrinking the distance between buyers and sellers. A recent Nielsen Global online survey[12] found that 85 percent of the world's online population uses the Internet to make purchases. In two years, the number of online shoppers has grown from 627 million to 875 million—a 40 percent increase. By country, the highest percentage of Internet users who shop online was found in South Korea (99 percent), followed by the United Kingdom (97 percent), Germany (97 percent), and Japan (97 percent). Although the United States came in eighth with 94 percent, it remained the largest and most established e-commerce marketplace by far, with e-commerce continuing to experience double-digit year-over-year growth in 2007. Forrester Research estimates that business-to-consumer (B2C) e-commerce in the United States will grow from $175 billion in 2007 to $335 billion by 2012.[13]

According to Nielsen, 60 percent of global online customers use credit cards for online purchases. Twenty-five percent use PayPal. Shopping online by credit card is especially appealing to consumers in emerging markets who cannot find items they want in their market, creating new opportunities for both retailers and consumers. Debit cards are another popular payment method in the United Kingdom and the United States, where 59 percent and 40 percent of online customers respectively use debit cards. Most online shoppers return to familiar sites. Therefore, it is important for companies to capture new Internet shoppers

12 Nielson Global Online Survey conducted October to November 2007, www.nielsen.com/media/2008/pr_080128b.html.

13 Sucharita Mulpuru, "US eCommerce Forecast: 2008 To 2012," Forrester Research, January 18, 2008, www.forrester.com/research/document/excerpt/0,7211,41592,00.html.

early and to hold on to them by ensuring a positive shopping experience. One-third of all online shoppers used a search engine or surfed on their own to find the best online stores. One in four shoppers relied on recommendations from fellow consumers. These tendencies reflect the importance to consumers of trust and confidence in the online environment. Personal information is key to virtually all business transactions, making issues of privacy, data protection, identity theft, and cross-border data flows central to the continued growth of e-commerce both in the United States and abroad.

The United States is well positioned to take advantage of these trends as the most networked large economy in the world. In April 2008, the World Economic Forum (WEF) moved the United States up three positions to the fourth most network-ready country in the world, behind only Denmark, Sweden, and Switzerland. The Networked Readiness Index looks at how countries use information and communications technology (ICT) in three ways: the presence of an ICT friendly and ICT conducive environment; the level of ICT readiness for individuals, businesses, and government; and the actual use of ICT by these stakeholders.[14] The Department of Commerce's January 2008 report, "Networked Nation: Broadband in America, 2007" shows that the Administration's technology, regulatory, and fiscal policies have stimulated innovation and competition, and encouraged investment in the U.S. broadband market. According to the Federal Communications Commission, as of December 2006, broadband service was available in 99 percent of the nation's ZIP codes, encompassing 99 percent of the nation's population. From December 2000 to December 2006, broadband lines in the United States grew by more than 1,100 percent, from about 6.8 million lines to 82.5 million lines.[15]

U.S. COMPETITIVENESS IN THE GLOBAL ECONOMY

America's strong economic foundations—flexible labor markets, sophisticated capital markets, low taxes, and open trade and investment policies—have kept the American economy

14 World Economic Forum, *The Global Information Technology Report 2007-2008* (Geneva: WEF, 2008), x.
15 U.S. Department of Commerce, National Telecommunications and Information Administration, "Networked Nation: Broadband in America", January 2008, www.ntia.doc.gov/reports/2008/NetworkedNation.html.

resilient during the current economic slowdown. These same fundamentals also give our exporters a competitive advantage in overseas markets. A wide range of independent measures validate American competitiveness in the global economy. Far from indicating weakness or decline, these measures continue to rank the United States at or near the top of all countries in the world.

TABLE 1

U.S. RANKINGS IN GLOBAL COMPETITIVENESS

	U.S. Ranking	Countries Ahead of the United States	Countries Immediately Behind the United States
Global Competitiveness Index 2007—2008 (WEF)	1		Switzerland Denmark Sweden Germany
Business Competitiveness Index 2007—2008 (WEF)	1		Germany Finland Sweden Denmark
Ease of Doing Business 2008 (World Bank)	3	Singapore New Zealand	Hong Kong Denmark United Kingdom Canada
Globalization Index 2007 (A.T. Kearney/Foreign Policy)	7	Singapore Hong Kong Netherlands Switzerland Ireland Denmark	Canada Jordan Estonia Sweden
Inward FDI Potential Index, results for 2003-2005 (UNCTAD)	1		Singapore United Kingdom Canada Luxembourg

Global Competitiveness Index (GCI): The WEF's GCI is a broad measure of a country's competitiveness based on an assessment of institutions, policies, and factors that determine its level of productivity. The GCI gives the United States the lead position. Based on the United States' highly sophisticated and innovative companies, efficient markets, excellent university system, and scale opportunities of a large domestic economy, WEF describes the United States as the country with the most productive and innovative potential in the world.[16]

Business Competitiveness Index (BCI): The WEF's BCI focuses on the business environment for individual companies. Again, the United States holds the first position. According to the BCI,[17] the United States' greatest strengths are its innovative capacity (university-industry collaboration, local availability of specialized research and training services, etc.) and financial markets (venture capital availability and financial market sophistication). Germany's runner-up ranking is attributed to the export orientation of its companies.

16 World Economic Forum, *Global Competitiveness Report,* 2007–2008 (Geneva: WEF, 2007) 12.
17 Ibid., 66.

Ease of Doing Business, 2008: The World Bank's Doing Business rankings measure factors essential to efficient business operation, including licenses, taxes, trade across borders, and contract enforcement. By this measure, the United States ranks third behind only Singapore and New Zealand. The United States scored high on starting a business (4), employing workers (1), getting credit (7), and low on paying taxes (76).[18]

Globalization Index 2007: *Foreign Policy* Magazine and A.T. Kearney's Globalization Index[19] measures a country's economic integration, personal contact, technological connectivity, and political engagement in the world. By this measure, the United States dropped four places to seventh from 2006 to 2007. While 12 percent trade growth was a positive sign of globalization, the measure pointed to shrinking foreign investment as a major negative.

Inward Foreign Direct Investment (FDI) Potential Index: The Inward FDI Index of the United Nations Conference on Trade and Development (UNCTAD) is an indication of the stability of a country's structural variables, including GDP per capita, infrastructure, education, exports, and inward FDI stock. On this basis, the United States has held the number one spot since the measure was first published in 1988.[20]

FOREIGN DIRECT INVESTMENT IN THE UNITED STATES

As indicated by this last measure, FDI—along with trade—is another critical component of the U.S. economy, itself contributing to productivity growth, U.S. exports, and high-paying jobs for American workers. More than 5 million Americans work in jobs created by foreign direct investment, and FDI accounts for 10 percent of U.S. capital investment, 15 percent of annual research and development expenditures, and 20 percent of U.S. exports. For these reasons, the United States welcomes foreign investment and provides international investors a stable and open economy, helping to make the country the world's largest recipient of foreign direct investment. In 2007 alone, the United States received $204 billion in FDI.[21] The total stock of FDI in the United States in 2006 was equivalent to 13.6 percent of U.S. GDP.[22] Most international investment in the United States originates from Organization for Economic Cooperation and Development (OECD) countries. In 2006 alone, approximately 70 percent of FDI inflows originated from Europe and Japan. Several emerging markets, however, are playing a growing role. Between 2002 and 2006, India's FDI position in the United States grew by a compound annual growth rate of 55 percent. This was followed by countries such as Russia (48 percent), Chile (41 percent), South Korea (24 percent), and Brazil (18 percent).[23]

Although the United States continues to be the largest recipient of FDI inflows, it has lost significant position in the global race for FDI. The U.S. share of FDI inflows has declined

18 World Bank, "Doing Business 2008" (summary data for the United States), www.doingbusiness.org/exploreeconomies/?economyid =197.

19 "The Globalization Index 2007," November/December 2007, *Foreign Policy Magazine,* www.foreignpolicy.com/story/cms. php?story_id=3995&print=1.

20 United Nations Conference on Trade and Development (UNCTAD), "Inward FDI Potential Index – Results for 2003-2005," www. unctad.org/Templates/wedflyer.asp?intitemid=2472&lang=1.

21 U.S. Department of Commerce, Bureau of Economic Analysis, "Balance of Payments (International Transactions)," www.bea.gov/ international/index.htm#bop.

22 U.S. Department of the Treasury, "An Open Economy is Vital to U.S. Prosperity," Fact Sheet, May 2007.

23 U.S. Department of Commerce, Bureau of Economic Analysis, "Operations of Multinational Companies," www.bea.gov/ international/index.htm#omc.

INAUGURAL "INVEST IN AMERICA" WEEK

In May 2008, Secretary of Commerce Carlos M. Gutierrez announced the inaugural *Invest in America Week*, May 5-9, 2008. A series of events in 12 states across the country highlighted the importance of foreign direct investment (FDI) for U.S. jobs and economic growth. These events took place in Arizona, California, Connecticut, Kentucky, Maryland, Massachusetts, Nevada, New Hampshire, New York, Pennsylvania, Rhode Island, and Wisconsin. The Department of Commerce created the *Invest in America* program in 2007 as the first Federal-level U.S. investment promotion effort in a generation. The program provides support for State governments' investment promotion efforts in all 50 States, U.S. territories, and the District of Columbia, and facilitates *Invest in America Week* activities to showcase the benefits of foreign investment in America.

Photo: Hitachi officials lead Secretary of Commerce Carlos M. Gutierrez and California Governor Arnold Schwarzenegger on a plant tour during Invest In America Week in May 2008.

from 31 percent of global FDI in 1980, to 13 percent in 2006.[24] Advanced and developing economies have recognized the value of foreign investment, resulting in an increasingly competitive international environment for FDI flows. All OECD members now maintain an investment promotion agency to attract foreign investment.

CONCLUSION

Several external factors have contributed to the success of U.S. exports in recent years, including the growth of foreign markets, changes in the terms of trade (i.e., exchange rates), and lower costs of conducting international business. Yet the most important factors driving U.S. exports are inherent to U.S. industry. An open and growing global economy plays to the strengths of U.S. industry as the most productive, innovative, and competitive in the world.

24 United Nations Conference on Trade and Development (UNCTAD), FDI Database, www.unctad.org/Templates/Page. asp?intItemID=1923&lang=1.

Broadening and Deepening the Base of Exporters

U.S. exporters registered another stellar year in 2007, with new records across a wide range of markets and sectors. However, the U.S. business community is just beginning to tap its export potential, with exporting companies representing a smaller percentage of the U.S. business community than they represent for our foreign competitors. With slowing economic growth at home and continued strong import demand abroad, now is the time for U.S. companies to expand into foreign markets. Our goal is to engage more U.S. companies than ever in the global marketplace, by raising awareness of export opportunities and assistance. The challenge is reaching potential exporters throughout the large and diverse U.S. business community of 27.2 million firms.[1] The solution is strategic partnerships among all stakeholders in the United States who share an interest in seeing our country continue to prosper through exports. The U.S. Government is also taking several concrete steps to make its services more accessible, especially for small companies and new exporters who most need help.

AMERICA'S EXPORT POTENTIAL

For four straight years, U.S. exports have grown at double-digit rates. With exports growing faster than the general economy, the share of the U.S. GDP accounted for by exports

1   Small Business Administration, Office of Advocacy, "Frequently Asked Questions," September 2008.

CHART 7
G7 MEMBER EXPORTS AS A PERCENTAGE OF GDP, 1990–2006

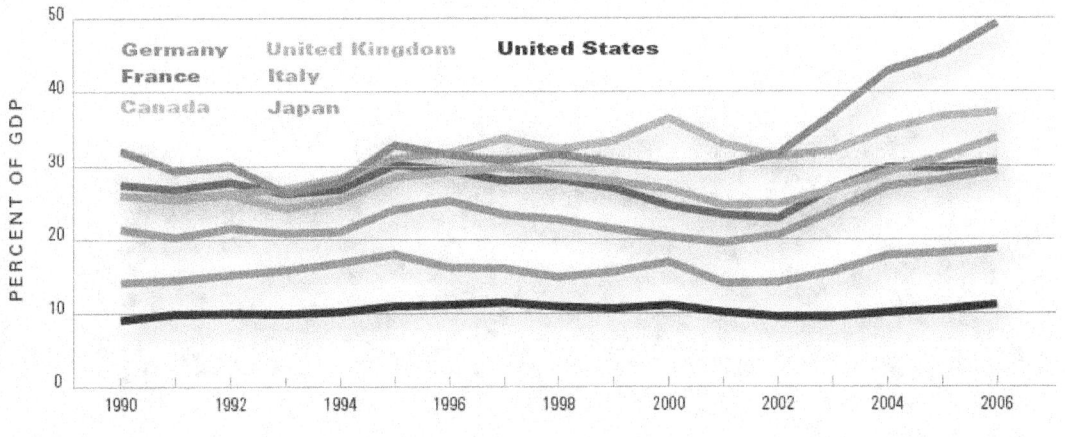

Note: Based on exports of goods and services and on GDP in current prices and purchasing power parity.

Source: Organization for Economic Cooperation and Development, *OECD Factbook 2008: Economic, Environmental, and Social Statistics.*

has steadily increased. In 2003, exports accounted for 9.5 percent of GDP. By 2007, exports accounted for a record 11.9 percent. Yet, exports have not yet broken out of the 9 to 12 percent range of the past 15 years, and compared to our major industrial competitors, exports remain a relatively low and flat share of the U.S. national economy. Chart 7 shows that exporting accounts for a higher share of GDP for competitors represented by the traditional Group of Seven (G7) industrial economies. More importantly, the role of exports in economic growth has grown significantly in recent years for most of our competitors. Exports now account for 49 percent of Germany's economy, up from 30 percent in 2001. Other competitors have seen similar—if less dramatic—trends in reaching new highs for the contribution of exports to economic activity, including large economies such as the United Kingdom (34 percent), France (30 percent), and Japan (19 percent).

The steadily increasing role of exports in the U.S. economy has also been evident in the growing share of the business community that is exporting. In 2006 (most recent data), the number of U.S. companies exporting grew 2.3 percent to 245,945 firms (*Chart 8*). Since 2002, the number of exporters has grown 10 percent and is just short of the pre-September 11 peak.

While the number of U.S. exporters—nearly 246,000—is impressive, it represents less than one percent of the 27.2 million businesses in the United States. In addition, the number of U.S. exporters has not kept pace with the overall growth of the business community. Since 1997, the number of all enterprises has grown 28 percent,[2] while the number of exporters has increased by only 15 percent. It is important to note that exporting is not a feasible pursuit for a large share of the U.S. business community. For example, certain service providers, such as barbershops, require proximity to their consumers and are not able to export their services across borders. Yet as the most innovative and productive nation on earth, the United States has tens of thousands of American small business manufacturers, wholesalers, and services sector firms that produce competitive goods and services, but do not export. Among our major industrial competitors, a much higher share of the enterprises export. While it is no surprise that a high percentage of companies export in small indus-

2 Small Business Administration, Office of Advocacy, Firm Size Data, www.sba.gov/advo/research/data.html. (Note: the figure was calculated from various data sources available at this website.)

CHART 8
NUMBER OF U.S. COMPANIES EXPORTING

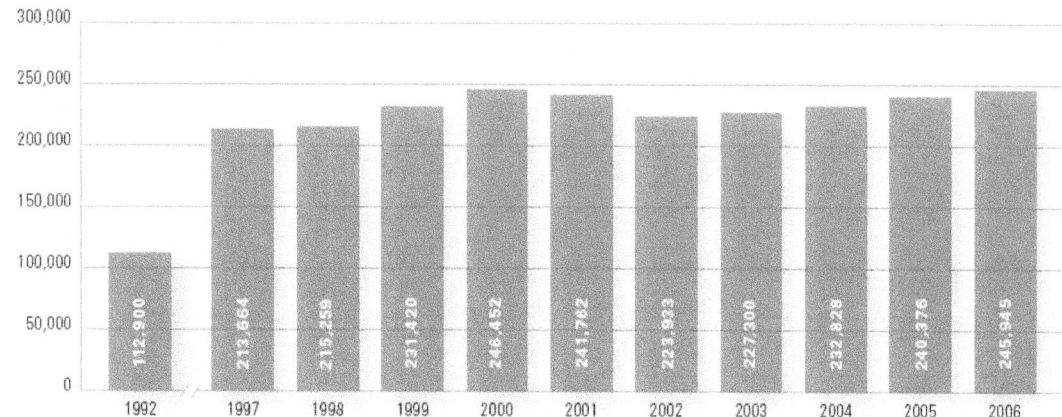

Note: Data are not available for 1993–1996.

Source: U.S. Department of Commerce, Bureau of the Census.

2008 NATIONAL EXPORT STRATEGY

FOREIGN COMPETITION AND TRADE PROMOTION ASSISTANCE

Most every competitor country we have reviewed identifies expansion of exporting opportunities for small and medium-sized enterprises (SMEs) as a national economic priority. The
European Union is concerned that only 8 percent of its SMEs export. European research
concludes that the number of exporters is the main determinant of their countries' exporting
base, and encourages governments to make broadening the number of exporters a priority.[*] France committed to increasing the number of SMEs exporting by 50 percent. Likewise,
Australia committed in 2002 to an ultimately successful campaign to double its SME exporters. Japan, South Korea, and neighboring Association of Southeast Asian Nations (ASEAN)
have similarly identified SME exporting as an important public objective.

Addressing the "SME gap" has also been a priority of the United States and a perennial priority of the National Export Strategy. The governments of our trading partners approach the
issue from different perspectives. Some subsidize financing and market entry programs for
new exporters. Others have created umbrella agencies that combine industry, finance, trade
policy, and trade promotion under one roof. None of these approaches is suited to the U.S.
style of governance, which looks to maximize and complement the role of public and private
partners. It is important to know, however, what we are up against in the competitive global
marketplace. Chart 9 below shows export promotion spending in relation to actual exports
for the United States and competitor governments, focusing on basic export assistance and
market entry services.

* Thierry Mayer and Gianmarco I.P. Ottaviano, *The Happy Few: The Internationalization of European Firms*, Bruegel Blueprint Series, 51.

CHART 9
ESTIMATED GOVERNMENT EXPORT PROMOTION SPENDING
OF THE U.S. AND SELECTED MAJOR TRADING PARTNERS

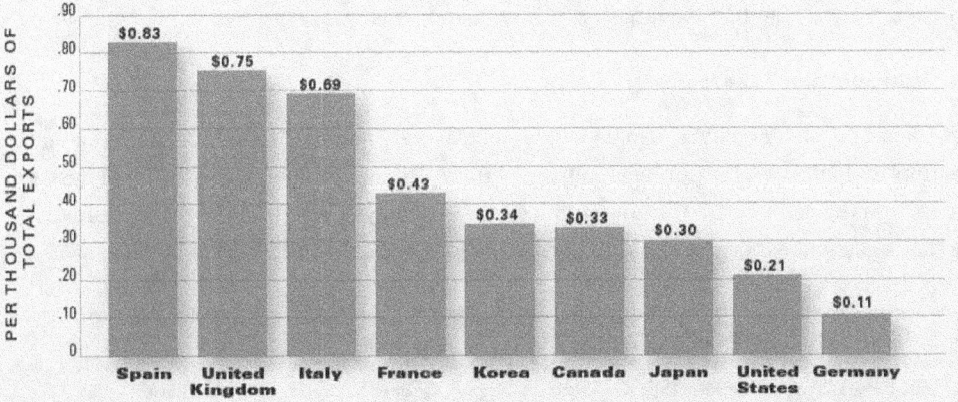

Note: Figures exclude trade financing and agricultural trade promotion.

Source: Foreign government sources, U.S. Commercial Service estimates, and World Trade Organization trade data.

trial European economies like Finland (19 percent) and Denmark (17 percent), we also see high participation in exporting in large economies, such as the United Kingdom (9 percent), Germany (9 percent), Italy (7 percent), and France (6 percent).[3] Outside of Europe, we know that 15 percent of Australian firms[4] and 8 percent of Canadian firms export.[5]

Profile of SME Exporters

Many forces drive trends in U.S. business participation in exporting from one year to the next, including foreign and domestic business cycles, exchange rates, and technology. However, to expand the base of exporters in the long term, we must first understand how the average U.S. company views the prospect of stepping into new and unfamiliar foreign markets. One important factor constraining the number of companies exporting is lack of information. The geographically large U.S. home market makes many U.S. companies complacent about export opportunities. Many companies focus exclusively on U.S. consumers, and therefore are not aware of global market opportunities. In addition, many companies have exaggerated perceptions of the risks and difficulties of exporting, and are not aware of risk mitigation strategies (including trade financing) and technological and logistical advances that make exporting cheaper and easier.

The good news is that 30 percent of non-exporters indicate they would consider exporting if they had more information on markets, specific opportunities, and the exporting process. The latest Census Bureau data indicates that:

- 97 percent of all exporting companies are SMEs.

- These SMEs account for 29 percent of U.S. exports by value.

- 90 percent of exporters conduct business from a single U.S. business location. Without overseas operations, SMEs have less access to information and are less able to overcome foreign trade barriers and market imperfections than larger companies with overseas operations or affiliates.

- 58 percent of exporters ship to only one foreign market, and as a group account for only 4.5 percent of the value of U.S. exports.

- Among the top 25 U.S. trading partners, the biggest percentage increases in the number of U.S. exporters were the United Arab Emirates (10 percent), India (10 percent), China (8 percent), and Brazil (6 percent).

- Belgium and Japan had the largest declines (2 and 1 percent respectively).[6]

New Metropolitan Export Data

Trade data by State and city is also becoming increasingly important for understanding our exporters and empowering our local outreach efforts. This information shows that States and cities across the country are thriving in the global economy. It also reinforces the positive role that trade and exports are having in creating jobs and growing local economies.

3 Gallup Organization, *Survey of the Observatory of European SMEs*, Flash EB Series #196, Fieldwork November 2006–January 2007 (Hungary: The Gallup Organization), 14-16.

4 Australian Trade Commission, "Small is Still Beautiful," August 15, 2007, www.austrade.gov.au/Small-is-still-beautiful/default.asp.

5 Statistics Canada, "Profile of Canadian Exporters," March 11, 2008, www.statcan.ca/Daily/English/080311/d080311c.htm.

6 U.S. Department of Commerce, Bureau of the Census, "A Profile of U.S. Exporting Companies, 2005–2006," news release January 11, 2008, www.census.gov/foreign-trade/Press-Release/edb/2006/edbrel.pdf.

"I love exporting because it has enabled me to meet so many people from other cultures. Exporting has made me more broad-minded, and I have developed a great appreciation for other cultures and the way others live their lives."
—Sharon Doherty, President

Vellus Products, a small maker of pet grooming products first became an exporter in 1993, when a Taiwanese businessperson bought $25,000 worth of the company's product to sell in Taiwan through dog shows. "I started receiving calls from people around the world who would hear of our products at dog shows and ask organizers how they could get in touch with me to buy our products," Doherty recalls. "But I needed a way to find market research and learn more about ways of doing business in these countries." By tapping the services of the Commercial Service, the U.S. Small Business Administration (SBA), and the State of Ohio, Vellus has expanded to 28 foreign markets. "As business has grown, I have gone from ordering country profiles to requesting customized export and financing strategies tailored to maximize export potential," Doherty says.

Photo: Sharon Doherty, President of Vellus Products, with a client's pet.

In January 2008, the Department of Commerce introduced a new data series that details U.S. merchandise export values by metropolitan area. The complete data series is located at www. trade.gov/metrodata. This new resource reveals that exports are having a positive impact on metropolitan economies. In 2006, 116 metropolitan areas recorded product sales of $1 billion or more. Other highlights include:

- In 2006, seven metropolitan areas posted export sales of $25 billion or more. These markets include New York–Northern New Jersey–Long Island; Houston–Sugar Land–Baytown; Los Angeles–Long Beach–Santa Ana; Seattle–Tacoma–Bellevue; Detroit–Warren–Livonia; Chicago–Naperville–Joliet; and San Jose–Sunnyvale–Santa Clara.

- An additional 30 metropolitan areas exported between $5 billion and $24 billion.

- These top 37 metropolitan areas accounted for 61 percent of total U.S. merchandise exports in 2006.

- A total of 290 metropolitan areas (79 percent) recorded positive growth in area exports between 2005 and 2006.

- Twenty-eight major metropolitan areas expanded exports by $1 billion or more between 2005 and 2006.

- Twenty-four other metropolitan areas posted 2005–2006 export increases between $500 million and $1 billion, while 89 more metropolitan areas registered export increases in the $100 million to $499 million range.

- Fifteen metropolitan areas accounted for at least 50 percent of their State's merchandise exports in 2006.

TPCC AGENCY INITIATIVES TO STRENGTHEN PARTNERSHIPS

Given slower economic growth at home, continued strong growth in emerging markets, and the increased price competitiveness abroad of U.S. goods and services, now is the time to capture the attention of a wider swath of the business community. Export promotion needs to become a greater concern of all stakeholders in the national economy. For these reasons, the Trade Promotion Coordinating Committee's (TPCC) Strategic Partnership Initiative continues to be the centerpiece of the National Export Strategy. The Strategic Partnership Initiative seeks to foster more cooperation among export service providers in both the public and private sectors. While the Federal Government provides important expertise and services, it lacks the resources, marketing channels, and points of contact with businesses to reach most U.S. companies. Only in collaboration with partners can we engage companies that have not yet explored their potential to export. At the same time, partners and potential exporters both expect U.S. Government services to keep pace with changing technology and customer expectations. The Federal Government must strive to make its services more accessible and affordable, especially for small companies and those new to exporting.

In the coming year, the TPCC agencies are committed to:

- Further expanding partnerships with cities and States, private corporations that provide export-related services, trade associations, and

- Providing greater access to U.S. Government export assistance, through better use of technology, outreach initiatives, and exporting tools.

Together, we can create a culture of exporting in America that helps to keep our industry competitive and our economy growing.

City and State-Level Strategic Partnerships

Across the country, States and cities have played an increasingly active role in promoting exports. Now, with the economy slowing at home, budgets are tightening at all levels of government. With exports playing a more important role than ever in our economic health and prosperity, however, export promotion is no longer a luxury. We encourage States, cities, and other localities to maintain their support for export programs. At the same time, together we must pursue new and innovative initiatives that unite stakeholders and excite the business community about trade. Together, we can dramatically expand awareness of exporting opportunities and the availability of export assistance. The U.S. Departments of Commerce and Agriculture and the Export-Import Bank of the United States (Ex-Im Bank), have expanded their programs for engaging more public sector partners. By highlighting these programs, as well as various models for cooperation and best practices, these agencies invite new States, cities, and other local governments to approach and engage them on trade.

U.S. Department of Commerce Models of Collaboration: The Commercial Service encourages its nationwide network of domestic U.S. Export Assistance Centers (USEACs) to engage States and cities on joint events and client assistance. The Commercial Service continues to strengthen strategic partnerships with national groups, such as the State International Development Organizations (SIDO). For example, with SIDO's help, we have incorporated course content and participants from the States into training programs designed to improve cross-governmental customer service and referrals.

Given the divergent resources available to exporters from one State or city to another, the Commercial Service must also take a customized approach to building cooperative export promotion strategies that leverage local resources while ensuring that the needs of all exporters are met. Over the past year, the Commercial Service has launched or expanded a number of such efforts with individual States and cities. While there is no standard operating model for effective local cooperation on trade promotion, the Commercial Service will work to engage an ever-widening circle of States and cities in these types of successful collaboration.

California: In 2005, the Commercial Service and California's Business, Transportation & Housing Agency created the California Trade Partnership. The partnership has supported trade missions led by Governor Arnold Schwarzenegger to Mexico, Canada, and China. In addition, the Commercial Service's Newport Beach office supported California's participation in the CeBIT Trade Fair—the world's largest information communications and technology trade show—in Hanover, Germany. The "California CeBIT Reception" has produced an increase in California's exposure to the European ICT market and promoted California as a leading hub for technology.

Connecticut: In May 2008, the Commercial Service in Middletown and a vast network of public and private sector partners launched the "New Global Main Street Challenge." The theme of the Challenge is recognition that Connecticut businesses are no longer the traditional manufacturers and services selling to the local "Main Street." They are innovative companies incorporating high technology solutions that are selling to—or seeking to sell to—global "Main Street" markets. Local and regional chambers and trade groups are recruiting local companies and supporting "How to Grow Your Business Internationally" events. Included in these events are "advocates" from Congress and State government promoting exporting to their constituencies. Challenge partners include the Connecticut District Export Council, the U.S. Small Business Administration (SBA), the Connecticut Business and Industry Association, the regional chambers of commerce, the Connecticut Department of Community and Economic Development, the University of Connecticut, and Junior Achievement. Over the next 12 months, Connecticut companies participating in the Challenge will be counseled, will participate in Commercial Service programs, and will be tracked for export successes.

Georgia: ExportGA, winner of the NASBITE [7] National Program Excellence Award, is a four-month, six-session workshop during which Georgia companies learn how to develop and expand successful export operations. Partners include the Commercial Service in Atlanta, the Georgia Department of Economic Development (GDeD), SBA, and the Small Business Development Center (SBDC). Participants are partnered with trade specialists from the Commercial Service and GDeD to incorporate each session's lesson into their export plans. During the final sessions, participants are already working with potential customers and skillfully implementing SBDC, SBA, and GDeD export services. Businesses had this to say about the program:

---

7 NASBITE International (formerly North American Small Business International Trade Educators).

"ExportGA has been the best consulting value in the world! I got company-specific coach-ing by an extensive team of State and Federal exporting professionals truly dedicated to helping me identify and secure profitable international sales."

—Michael Welch, Marketing Director, Welding Services, Inc.

"ExportGA has a level of professionalism and commitment that is exceptional. The Program has contributed to our entry into the Netherlands, Italy, Sweden, and Turkey, as well as increasing sales in the United Kingdom and Canada. It also helped clarify legal issues in Germany and gave us an understanding of CE marking[8] for our packaging. As a result, we've had an international sales increase of 47.6 percent!"

—Nicole Norris, International Marketing Manager, Gould Plastics, Inc.

"ExportGA lowered our export business start-up costs dramatically by tapping into the vast expertise and data base resources of the U.S. Export Assistance Center and Georgia Department of Economic Development. ExportGA helped me make contacts in my initial target market, Mexico, that directly resulted in sales there."

—Marvin Arentsen, President, D.A. Technologies, Inc.

Indiana: The Commercial Service's Export Assistance Center in Indiana and the Indiana Economic Development Corporation (IEDC) have joined together to promote small business participation in international trade shows through the Trade Show Assistance Program (TSAP). IEDC assists small Indiana business participation in shows recommended by the Commercial Service or the U.S. Department of Agriculture's (USDA) Foreign Agricultural Service (FAS).

North Dakota: The partnership between the Commercial Service office in North Dakota and the State of North Dakota Trade Office (NDTO) has helped North Dakota increase exports from $1.5 billion in 2006 to $2 billion in 2007, a 34 percent increase. With the Commercial Service's international trade expertise and global network, and the NDTO's coordinating role for trade education events and trade missions, the partnership has realized a number of recent successes. In September 2007, the NDTO and the Commercial Service brought over 100 foreign buyers from the Newly Independent States (of the former Soviet Union) to the Big Iron Farm Machinery Show in West Fargo. The foreign buyers were provided with tours and demonstrations of American farming practices, such as a Brandt Holdings-sponsored "Ride-N-Drive" event where they were able to drive John Deere equipment and ask questions about its features (see photo). In the six months following the trade show, U.S. companies exhibit-ing at the show sold approximately $14 million in U.S. farm machinery to visiting foreign buyers. In 2008, the partnership developed a winning proposal for a three-year International Trade Administration (ITA) Market Development Cooperator Program (MDCP) grant for the NDTO to establish an office in Ukraine, one of the most promising markets for North Dakota farm machinery exports. The partnership also organized trade missions to Taiwan, Ukraine, Russia, Kazakhstan, Australia, and South Korea.

West Virginia: The partnership between the State of West Virginia and the Commercial Service ensures that companies receive assistance from whichever organization is in the best position to help. This approach builds confidence in the programs and generates return customers. Every year, the State and the Commercial Service create a joint plan for trade

---

8   The CE marking (an acronym for the French "Conformité Européenne") certifies that a product has met EU health, safety, and environmental requirements.

North Dakota agricultural machinery companies such as Brandt Holdings (pictured above) welcomed agricultural machinery buyers to the Big Iron Farm Machinery Show in September 2007. The sign reads in Russian: "We Welcome International Visitors to the Pre-Owned Agricultural Equipment Presentation of Brandt Holdings Company."

missions, shows, and outreach programs to cultivate affordable, efficient, and appropriate methods for the rural and mostly small businesses in the State to expand and grow their international sales. At the core of the partnership is West Virginia's Gold Key Trade Mission program, through which West Virginia companies receive a comprehensive basket of services from the State and Federal partners, allowing them to markedly reduce the time, effort, and cost of generating sales in a new market. During these missions, West Virginia provides funding and logistics planning, while the Commercial Service provides staff expertise and market research, making these events appealing to both new and experienced exporters.

Recent City- and State-Led Trade Missions and Shows: State, city, and local government leaders are playing a growing role in raising business awareness of trade and in creating more opportunities for companies to visit foreign markets and meet foreign buyers. The personal involvement of governors and mayors is playing an invaluable role in encouraging businesses to take the step of becoming active exporters.

West Virginia Governor's Trade Mission to China: In November 2007, the State of West Virginia brought together several of its key economic development partnering organizations to coordinate a Governor's Trade Mission to China. The mission included 11 small companies plus representatives from the West Virginia Coal Association, the Discover the Real West Virginia Foundation, West Virginia University, and the West Virginia Development Office. Commercial Service support helped to ensure a successful event. The highlight of the trade mission was the China Coal & Mining Expo in Beijing, which the State of West Virginia has sponsored since 1999. Eleven West Virginia companies exhibited at this show in 2007. The

West Virginia Governor Joe Manchin, III (left); Dr. Zhang Yuzhuo, Senior Vice President of Shenhua Group Corporation Ltd. (middle); and Dr. Qingyun Sun, Associate Director of the U.S.—China Energy Center at West Virginia University (right) at the Shenhua Group's Direct Coal Liquification Pilot Project in Shanghai, November 1, 2007.

participation of West Virginia companies in the show helped the Expo organizers satisfy the criteria to attain the designation as a U.S. Department of Commerce Certified Trade Show beginning in 2005.

South Carolina's First Annual Global Business Forum: More than 140 individuals participated in the April 2007 Global Business Forum at the Columbia Metropolitan Convention Center, the first such event sponsored by the nine organizations of the South Carolina International Trade Coalition (SCITC). The SCITC includes the Commercial Service offices in Greenville, Columbia, and Charleston; the City of Columbia; the Export Consortium; the South Carolina Departments of Commerce and Agriculture; the South Carolina Forestry Commission; the South Carolina World Trade Center; the South Carolina State Ports Authority; and the South Carolina District Export Council. The all-day event focused on Canada, Mexico, Central America, Australia, Vietnam, and China. In addition to having local leaders speak and exhibit, the Commercial Service in Hanoi participated live via Internet broadcast. Public and private officials from South Carolina's Upstate and Low Country areas participated in order to replicate the event in Greenville and Charleston, South Carolina.

New Orleans Trade and Investment Mission to Honduras and Costa Rica: The Louisiana Economic Department (LED), the Commercial Service in New Orleans, and the Louisiana District Export Council organized a successful trade and investment mission to Honduras and Costa Rica from November 12–17, 2007. The delegation focused on the transportation, logistics, tourism, and education sectors, and included representatives of New Orleans

International Airport, the Port of South Louisiana, Louisiana State University, Nicholls State University, Pan American Insurance, the City of New Orleans, the State of Louisiana, and health care and building material companies. Louisiana—and particularly New Orleans—has long been oriented toward Latin American markets. With the recent Central America-Dominican Republic-United States Free Trade Agreement (CAFTA-DR) and planned expansion of the Panama Canal, this relationship is expected to become even stronger. Results to date include several tourism successes, a Honduran company's interest in a warehouse and distribution facility in New Orleans, and university student recruitment leads.

Louisiana Gulf Coast Oil Exposition (LAGCOE): Held in Lafayette, Louisiana in October 2007, LAGCOE exemplifies what Federal, State and city government, private industry, and non-profit organizations can accomplish when they team up to work together toward a common goal. The biennial LAGCOE show is the second largest and oldest oil and gas industry trade event in the United States. With the 2005 show cancelled due to hurricanes Katrina and Rita, collaboration on the 2007 event was imperative. The Commercial Service organized a successful "Showtime" program and international seminar series, bringing in eight delegations of 175 buyers from oil-rich countries. The State of Louisiana provided assistance to the show organizers for marketing and promotion. The City of Lafayette provided daily transportation for international visitors and set up the International Business Center and Lounge. The Lafayette Economic Development Authority helped host a reception for visitors.

Los Angeles Trade Mission to India: The Los Angeles County Economic Development Corporation (LAEDC) and its subsidiary, the World Trade Center Association Los Angeles-Long Beach, and the Commercial Service in Los Angeles organized a 25-member trade mission to New Delhi, Mumbai, and Kolkata, India from March 2–9, 2008. The delegation included representatives from the cities of Long Beach and Los Angeles, the Port of Long Beach, Los Angeles World Airports, and representatives from major corporations including AECOM, Clean Energy, CSULB, KPMG, and Paramount. The preliminary reports from participating companies include over $70 million in projected export sales, as well as possible future business with major Indian airlines and hotels.

U.S. Department of Agriculture Work with States Groups: USDA works with States and other local governments through outreach and education, as well as to deliver agricultural services.

NCSL Dialogue: Through a partnership with the National Conference of State Legislators (NCSL) since 1999, FAS has provided outreach and support to State legislators and policy makers about agricultural exports, trade agreements, and the FAS. The partnership has promoted a national dialogue on agricultural trade with State legislators supporting legislator travel on State foreign agricultural marketing trips (e.g., an Alabama State legislator delegation to India in 2007); an annual national legislative agricultural summit for the States (held in Washington, D.C. in 2007); and roundtables on agricultural issues at NCSL annual meetings (held in Boston in 2007). The partnership provides State legislatures with technical assistance, research and analysis of legislative proposals, and the tracking of State laws related to trade. The partnership also identifies critical issues and current trends in agricultural trade policies.

State Regional Trade Groups (SRTGs): The SRTGs have helped to expand U.S. export opportunities by creating thousands of business contacts between foreign buyers and U.S. suppliers. The SRTGs have worked with hundreds of companies to promote value-added products in more than 65 countries, and have sponsored hundreds of promotional and exporter assistance events with USDA support. In 2007, more than 65 outreach events were conducted by the four SRTGs and attended by hundreds of established and new-to-export companies.

Ex-Im Bank City/State Partners Program: The City-State Partners Program is a nationwide marketing initiative that brings State and local government offices and private-sector organizations into partnerships with Ex-Im Bank to expand export opportunities. Since 2007, Ex-Im Bank has expanded participation in its City/State Partners Program by 20 percent with the addition of nine new partners. Ex-Im Bank now has 53 partners in 31 States and the Commonwealth of Puerto Rico. Recent additions to the program include partners in major U.S. cities such as Los Angeles and New York City. In July 2007, the Los Angeles Area Chamber of Commerce became a Partner to help local businesses learn about and apply for a range of Ex-Im Bank financing products, including short-term export-credit insurance to mitigate the risk of foreign buyer nonpayment; loan guarantees to increase export-related working capital; and medium-term financing for foreign buyers. The Chamber has worked since 1888 to improve the economy and quality of life of the Los Angeles region. In April 2008, Ex-Im Bank partnered with the Brooklyn International Trade Development Center (BITDC) to help companies in the greater New York City metropolitan area get the financing they need. BITDC was established in 2006 at the Medgar Evers College of the City University of New York to promote the expansion of the local economy through increased international trade in goods and services and related activities, with the overall goal of workforce development and job creation.

Corporate Partnerships

A growing priority for the trade promotion agencies is working with large services corporations whose millions of clients represent tens of thousands of potential exporters. A surprisingly large variety of such companies have a shared interest with the U.S. Government in seeing their own clients broaden and deepen their exporting activities. These partners and potential partners can include providers of shipping, logistics, warehousing, banking, e-business solutions, Internet marketing, and legal assistance. Moreover, these companies make available to their clients the very latest in U.S. innovation, technology, and customer service directed at helping companies transact foreign business successfully. The Department of Commerce, Overseas Private Investment Corporation (OPIC), and SBA continue to seek additional private-sector partners and the deepening of relationships and activities with current partners.

U.S. Department of Commerce's Corporate Partnership Program: The Commercial Service's Corporate Partnership Program continues to break new ground and is proving to be an effective mechanism for engaging the SME community. The force multiplier effect that companies such as UPS, FedEx, and Google generate, combined with the targeted marketing efforts of regional banks such as PNC and M&T, represents an integrated and comprehensive outreach effort.

The intention is to create a "Best of Class Partnership Program" where there is a partner (nationally and regionally) in every step of the exporting process—education, business development, international marketing, market intelligence, business partner identification, and due diligence—as well as in those industry segments that are stakeholders in international trade: finance, logistics, Internet portals, publishing, shipping, travel, and lodging.

To that end, the Commercial Service has added six new partners in 2008: Baker and McKenzie, LLP; City National Bank; Comerica Bank; TD Bank; the United States Postal Service; and Zions Bank (See Profiles, p. 27). The new partners are consistent with the rationale stated above and expand the Commercial Service's reach, on a national and regional basis, to the SME community.

As the program matures, its effect on the Commercial Service's ability to reach the SME community is profound. By leveraging the private sector's sales and marketing expertise, the Commercial Service is becoming more relevant than ever to the SME community, and is at the forefront of the movement to create a "Culture of Exporting" in the U.S. business community.

The positive effects of the relationships are mutually reinforcing to the Commercial Service in the following ways:

Branding: Partnerships increase brand awareness of the Commercial Service and its programs and services among all stakeholders.

Export Promotion: Partnerships increase the visibility of exporting as a viable business development strategy.

Expanding Marketing Channels: Partnerships provide additional marketing channels to reach SMEs that are not exporting or that are exporting to only one market. Commercial Service information on new trade opportunities and market trends is available to a wider audience.

Innovative Advertising: Partnering enables the Commercial Service to participate in innovative advertising and marketing programs of world-class U.S. companies.

Trade Mission Promotion: Partnerships provide a new channel for marketing the Certified Trade Missions program.

Enhanced Services: By leveraging the resources and expertise of the partner, Commercial Service trade specialists—both domestic and international—better understand the export process and can deliver a better service to existing and new clients.

We know from partner metrics that our joint marketing efforts are generating more international sales for SMEs, clearly supporting the rationale of strategic partnerships as a force multiplier. The number of contacts with an SME—whether it is by attending an event, a sales call made by the private sector partner promoting exporting, an article in a partner's monthly newsletter, or website referrals—are all relevant in gauging the performance of the Corporate Partnership Program. In 2007, corporate partners spent an estimated $3 to $4 million to sup-

One of the examples of how the Commercial Service's Corporate Partnership Program has delivered concrete, measurable results is a series of seminars titled "The Web Revolution for Business," held in seven major cities across the United States. This half-day program featured speakers from three of the partners: Google, FedEx, and Baker & McKenzie. Google speakers covered the topic of how to increase international sales and attract Web site visitors by using free Internet-based tools and design methods. FedEx speakers demonstrated the resources available to exporters to navigate through customs clearance, understand export documentation requirements, manage a supply chain, and save both time and money when shipping internationally. Baker & McKenzie attorneys discussed the global legal framework that affects Web site design, e-commerce, international marketing, and customer relationship management via the Web. These seminars provided the tools and information necessary for companies to expand their businesses globally with less risk, lower cost, and better efficiency.

port the partnership program with the Commercial Service—more than double the Commercial Service's entire marketing budget, including personnel. Partnership activities generated:

- 3,272,529 contacts with SMEs;

- 198,184 referrals from partner Web sites to Export.gov.

The Commercial Service will continue to support a strong Corporate Partnership Program to help create a "Culture of Exporting" that ultimately begins to positively impact the total number of U.S. companies exporting in the United States. This is the ultimate goal of the Corporate Partnership Program.

OPIC Enterprise Development Network: In June 2007, OPIC launched the Enterprise Development Network (EDN), a strategic alliance with the private sector that greatly expands OPIC's ability to provide financing and political risk insurance to U.S. micro, small, and medium-sized enterprises (MSMEs) doing business in developing countries. Through the support of financial institutions, business consultants, associations, law firms, and regional investment promotion agencies, EDN eases MSMEs' access to OPIC products and services. By empowering such private-sector service providers, the network delivers services to American businesses more efficiently and cost-effectively, improving access to the kind of credit for overseas projects that is often difficult to obtain. It also unlocks an entirely new niche market for lenders and other service providers, offering them a valuable opportunity to expand their client bases into emerging markets overseas and a new means to service those clients by decreasing capital requirements for their financing.

EDN consists of three types of service providers: EDN loan and insurance **originators**, which help MSMEs to prepare OPIC applications, enhance market strategies, and draft or refine business plans; EDN **designated lenders**, financial institutions that establish OPIC-backed lending facilities that provide loans to MSMEs or their affiliates for projects in OPIC-eligible countries; and EDN **advisers**, specialists in particular business sectors and geographic areas who assist OPIC in credit underwriting and due diligence on OPIC-funded loans. In June

TD Bank

Following TD Bank Financial Group's acquisition of Commerce Bancorp Inc. on March 31, 2008, it was announced that operations of TD Banknorth and Commerce Bank would be combined under the brand name TD Bank, America's Most Convenient Bank*.

- Commerce Bank is a retailer of financial services with more than 470 stores in New Jersey; New York; Connecticut; Pennsylvania; Delaware; Washington, D.C.; Virginia; Maryland; and Florida.

- TD Banknorth and Commerce Bank form one of the 20 largest commercial banking organizations in the United States, with over $109 billion in assets. They provide customers with a full range of financial products and services at nearly 1,100 locations from Maine to Florida. TD Banknorth, Commerce Bank, and TD Bank are trade names of TD Bank, N.A.

U.S. Postal Service

- Serves more than 9 million customers daily at nearly 37,000 retail locations and has annual operating revenue of nearly $75 billion ($2.0 billion in international shipments).

- Has one of the world's largest e-mail systems, delivering more than 13 million e-mails a day with an average delivery time of less than 5 seconds.

- Delivered 3.6 billion e-mail messages in 2007. This amount has been growing at a rate of 35 percent per year.

- Does not receive tax dollars for operations. Is a self-supporting agency, using the revenue from the sale of postage, products, and services to pay expenses.

City National Bank

- Headquartered in Los Angeles, City National is backed by nearly $16 billion in total assets.

- Domestic network consists of 62 offices, including 15 regional centers located in California, Nevada, and New York City.

- Specializes in commercial lending, private banking, cash management, international banking, and wealth management.

- A delegated authority lender of the Export-Import Bank of the United States and capable of providing government-backed working capital to domestic companies seeking to export their products and services.

Baker & McKenzie

- Baker & McKenzie has a global network of 3,600 attorneys located in 70 locations throughout 38 countries.

- Provides expertise in international trade regulation and corporate compliance for most commercially significant countries in the world, including customs laws and trade regulation; export controls and anti-boycott regulations; and antidumping and countervailing duty law.

Zions Bank

- A subsidiary of Zions Bancorporation, which has more than $50 billion in assets and is headquartered in Salt Lake City.

- Domestic network consists of more than 500 offices and 600 ATMs in 10 Western States: Arizona, California, Colorado, Idaho, Nevada, New Mexico, Oregon, Texas, Utah, and Washington.

- Specializes in foreign currency, trade finance, and management.

Comerica Bank

- A subsidiary of Comerica Incorporated, which has assets in excess of $67 billion and is based in Dallas.

- Domestic network consists of more than 400 banking centers in the United States in Michigan, California, Arizona, Texas, and Florida; and international offices in Canada, Mexico, and China.

- Provides a broad spectrum of financial services, including trust and international trade, export financing, and cash management.

2007, Wells Fargo HSBC Trade Bank was announced as an EDN designated lender through an agreement with OPIC to establish a $100 million lending facility. In addition, 14 organizations have agreed to serve as EDN loan originators: African Investment Corporation, LLC; Bank of Alameda; CEO Advisors; Delphos International, Ltd.; EPS Capital Corp.; Fidelity Indemnity (Pty) Limited; Florida Export Finance Corporation; Interlink Capital Strategies; GDI Financial Partners, LLC; MCDRS, LLC; METRIC, Inc.; Onfe, Inc.; Project Finance Advisors, LLC; and Terra Vista Capital, Inc. Since the launch in June 2007, OPIC has continued to add EDN partners, including two new loan originators. The African Investment Corporation (AiC), based in Bethesda, Maryland, is an international consulting company that promotes foreign direct investment in African countries. Wambia Capital, based in Washington, D.C., is an investment and risk advisor with expertise in African capital markets.

SBA Expansion of the Preferred Lender Program (PLP): In a move to boost lending to small businesses engaged in international trade, SBA has expanded its Preferred Lender Program (PLP). This measure will make it easier for small businesses to apply for—and for banks to process—loans for the agency's primary international loan program. Under the PLP, SBA delegates to the lender the authority to apply an SBA guarantee, up to 90 percent, up to $2 million. SBA does not have to review the application before the lender's approval of the loan and guarantee.

This program is the most financially effective tool SBA has to provide transaction financing for small businesses seeking to expand into international markets. Granting PLP lenders this authority will enhance small companies' access to capital. "For our Nation's small businesses to aggressively compete in the global marketplace, they need financing, access to capital," said former SBA Administrator Steve Preston. "As we extend this program to lenders, we make that access easier, more transparent, and help small businesses grow, which in turn grows our economy. We encourage PLP lenders to join us in this effort."

Trade Associations and Other Non-Profit Organizations

An important third category of strategic partner is non-profit trade groups that represent not only unique access to potential exporters, but also valuable expertise on sectors, foreign markets and issues. Most trade associations and business groups are already in the business of providing member services. As exporting becomes more and more important to the future competitiveness of all industry sectors, we encourage trade associations to bolster their trade awareness and assistance efforts in partnership with the TPCC agencies. SBA, OPIC, and the Departments of Agriculture, State, and Commerce will continue to build on recent joint activities as well as implement new initiatives in the coming year to leverage these important force multipliers.

Small Business Administration Work with Resource Partners: SBA supports a broad network of resource partners with business know-how, ranging from retired business executives to lawyers to instructors at universities and education centers. SBA is actively reaching out to these groups to increase awareness of the growing importance of exporting to many of their clients.

Small Business International Trade Symposiums: In April 2008, SBA and the Association of Small Business Development Centers (ASBDC) presented the inaugural Small Business International Trade Symposium in Hialeah, Florida, outside of Miami. This was the first of a national series of symposiums designed to provide information on accessing services to support business exports, educate small businesses on the opportunities created by U.S. free trade agreements, and to celebrate the role and contribution of small businesses in international trade. The business audience of nearly 400 participated in a Town Hall meeting with Secretary of Commerce Gutierrez and former SBA Administrator Preston, learned strategies for global trade from successful small business exporters, and discovered practical opportunities for taking advantage of free trade agreements from senior U.S. commercial officers stationed abroad. The Symposium was also a model of local collaboration between partners, with the event co-hosted by the City of Hialeah, and with the south Florida USEACs, the Florida District Export Council, and the Enterprise Florida consortium of State-wide assistance services all playing a critical role in making the event a success. Additionally, private partners, including SunTrust Bank, FedEx, and the Jay Malina International Trade Consortium, played an important role in cosponsoring the event and helping to promote it.

TPCC International Trade Certificate Course: A task force comprised of the SBA, the Department of Commerce, the ASBDC, and several individual SBDCs developed the first-ever full-day TPCC International Trade Certificate Course presented at the ASBDC Annual Conference September 2–5, 2008, in Chicago, Illinois. The more than 1,000 SBDCs nationwide provide small businesses with management and technical assistance. Some 35 of these centers are designated as International Trade Centers. The course is aimed primarily at those SBDC counselors who otherwise do not have significant international trade experience. The overall goal is to align with the National Export Strategy's focus on partnerships to reach more businesses and broaden the base of exporters. Four sessions cover: identifying export readiness and market and partner selection; international trade finance; what free trade agreements mean to small business; and understanding and utilizing TPCC government-wide resources. Speakers for the course also participate in the ASBDC International Interest Section Meeting to discuss future projects and goals.

OPIC Partners Program: The Partners Program is a public diplomacy initiative dedicated to expanding knowledge of the role of OPIC as the primary U.S. Government agency supporting private-sector investment in emerging markets. The focus of the program is to work with key organizations throughout the United States to create a greater understanding of OPIC's programs and activities. Partners include a wide range of trade associations; national, regional, and local business development councils and chambers; and other non-profit organizations.

U.S. Department of Agriculture Support of Trade Organizations and Trade Events: For nearly five decades, USDA's Foreign Agricultural Service (FAS) has partnered with food and agricultural industry organizations to develop markets overseas that remain vitally important to U.S. farmers and ranchers and an important source of income for food processing companies, transportation, and related industries. USDA market development programs support the efforts of U.S. companies and industries to build and maintain commercial markets in more than 100 countries for hundreds of food and agricultural products. These programs have fostered an effective trade promotion partnership between USDA and agricultural producers and processors who are represented by non-profit commodity or trade associations. That partnership is focused on capitalizing on opportunities to access new markets and reach new customers around the world. FAS' 80 overseas offices support industry efforts—especially in developing markets—by providing market intelligence and by introducing U.S. exporters to potential foreign customers.

MAP Activity: The Market Access Program (MAP) assists U.S. producers, exporters, private companies, and non-profit trade organizations in their promotional activities. Activities financed include consumer promotions, market research, technical assistance, and trade servicing. Working with industry organizations, FAS encourages outreach efforts that focus on facilitating export readiness for U.S. exporters. Small companies may also receive assistance from FAS on a cost-share basis through these nonprofit trade organizations and four State regional trade groups.

The MAP and Foreign Market Development Program are public-private partnerships administered by USDA to boost the overall level of market development.[9] As a result, total partnership spending has grown 150 percent in the past decade to more than $500 million (2007 projection). This growth is largely due to sharp increases in industry contributions (up 222 percent). On average, there has been a $10 return to economic welfare for each additional government dollar expended and a $5 return for each total government and industry dollar expended.

Trade Shows: In 2007, more than 910 U.S. companies participated in 30 FAS-endorsed trade shows overseas, making more than 9,200 serious trade contacts, reporting on-site sales totaling $54.9 million, and projecting estimated 12-month sales of $772 million. More than 3,900 new products were introduced in various markets. The FAS has successfully transferred overall management of most U.S. pavilions at international food shows to private sector partners, allowing FAS to scale back significantly its own staff and financial commitments while still supporting high-quality and effective trade events. FAS International Trade Shows in 2007 targeted several TPCC priority markets, including the United Arab Emirates (Gulf Food '07), China (SIAL China '07, F&H China Shanghai), Russia (World Food Moscow '07), and Vietnam (F&H Vietnam '07).[10]

USAEDC Activity: The U.S. Agricultural Export Development Council (USAEDC) is a non-profit private-sector trade association with approximately 80 members who are U.S. commodity trade associations, farmer cooperatives, and State regional trade groups from around the country.[11] They represent the interest of growers and processors of a variety of U.S. agricultural products. While privately funded, the councils cooperate closely with USDA's FAS. Promotional and development activities include market research, trade missions, reverse trade teams, literature, trade shows, in-store promotions, and ongoing evaluations. Members work with foreign governments; farm, manufacturing and importing organizations; and end users in various USDA programs that directly benefit both U.S. farmers and foreign consumers of U.S. agricultural exports. FAS annually partners with more than 75 trade organizations to stimulate demand for U.S. agricultural products in more than 100 countries. These partner-

9 www.fas.usda.gov/mos/programs/map.asp.

10 www.fas.usda.gov/scripts/agexport/EventQuery.asp.

11 www.usaedc.org

ships have resulted in agricultural export sales of more than $81 billion in 2007, and projected sales of $101 billion for Fiscal Year 2008.

U.S. Department of State Training Initiatives: The Department of State and other TPCC agencies continue to partner with the Business Council for International Understanding (BCIU) on a wide range of activities, from training to organization of major international trade and investment conferences.

Consultations for Ambassadors: Since its inception in 1955, BCIU has worked closely with the State Department to organize consultations for U.S. ambassadors with American business executives to discuss the commercial and economic environment, the U.S. corporate social responsibility programs, and initiatives for commercial diplomacy. Consultations are conducted in New York, Washington, Houston, Miami, London, and other cities.

Commercial Diplomacy Training: The BCIU Commercial Diplomacy Training Program enhances the trade literacy of the U.S. Foreign Service and U.S. and Foreign Commercial Service, as well as the efficacy of officers in other U.S. Government trade promotion agencies. The program is delivered year-round at the Foreign Service Institute and at other locations in the U.S. for political, economic, and commercial officers. In 2007, BCIU trained more than 500 officers serving in 127 countries around the world. The training program consists of week-long comprehensive training courses on the principles of commercial diplomacy, short introductory modules on commercial advocacy, and specialized seminars on key industry sectors such as infrastructure, information and communications technologies, innovative healthcare, and renewable energy. Additionally, BCIU organizes training for regional and country desk officers and for staff at American Presence Posts.

TPCC Interagency Training: BCIU conducts the TPCC Interagency Trade Officer Training Program for the Commerce Department and several other partner agencies, including the

Departments of State and Agriculture, Ex-Im Bank, OPIC, and SBA. The program helps both Federal and State business development staff to better gauge their customers' needs, deliver customized solutions, and leverage the resources of other agencies. Now in its sixth year, the program focuses on the real-world application of Federal Government assistance to drive successful export marketing campaigns for U.S. companies, especially SMEs. Participants learn how to package and seamlessly deliver more effective, customized solutions that integrate services from throughout the Federal Government. Through 2008, 640 participants from more than 12 Federal agencies and seven States had completed the four-day curriculum.

Corporate Practicum: The Foreign Service Institute's Economic Studies Program, with assistance from the Business Council for International Understanding (BCIU), supports a business practicum program that places Foreign Service Officers in companies for three to six months. This program cements officers' understanding of business challenges in international markets and exposes them to the methodologies and techniques of U.S. businesses operating internationally. Companies that have participated in the program include Boeing, BP, Caterpillar, GE Capital, GSK, Johnson and Johnson, and Raytheon. The program has been warmly received by the business community; in the words of Caterpillar: "The State Department practicum program has been very beneficial to Caterpillar because it allows Foreign Service Officers to work on projects involving the challenges and opportunities in cross-border commercial issues, and to interface with a large number of company managers who, in turn, learn more about the mission of—and support available from—the State Department."

U.S. Department of Commerce Grassroots Engagement: The Commercial Service works with a wide range of business groups at the local and national level. By playing an active role in these groups at the local level, the Commercial Service stays abreast of business concerns and interests. By working with national trade associations, the Commercial Service can reach more companies with specific business opportunities while benefiting from the expertise these associations represent.

District Export Councils (DEC): The Department of Commerce's closest private sector partners locally are the DECs, which consist of leaders from the local business community, appointed by the Secretary of Commerce. Currently there are 56 DECs with 1,500 exporters and private and public export service providers as members. On November 7–9, 2007, Commercial Service, the DECs, and the U.S. Chamber of Commerce convened the 2007 National DEC Conference titled "The Great Debate: The Future of U.S. Trade." More than 350 companies, trade organizations, and government representatives attended, making it the best-attended conference in years. The DECs are constantly creating or supporting new ways to reach out to business and bring together trade resources locally for the benefit of exporters. One of the most innovative outreach efforts this past year was the "Export University" series piloted in September 2007 by the Florida DEC to better equip SMEs to take advantage of the entire U.S. Government export arsenal. These one-day seminars bring representatives from across the U.S. Government together to instruct small and medium-sized companies on opportunities to expand their exporting business.

The DEC Trade Policy Committee is focused on increasing the amount of international education and foreign language initiatives within the U.S. public school system at the K–12 level, with particular emphasis on the language and cultures of Asian and Middle Eastern countries that are emerging as significant trade powers. Alliances in this initiative have been developed and will be developed with organizations, societies, and educational institutions which share this objective.

In addition, the Committee is developing a mentoring program that will match experienced international executives from large multinational organizations to SMEs so as to assist those SMEs in penetrating promising foreign markets, while at the same time avoiding pitfalls that might discourage smaller companies from exploring foreign opportunities.

New Association Bulletin: In December 2007, the Commercial Service launched an Association Bulletin e-mail to keep associations apprised of news and notices on Commercial Service activities. Of special note is the Commercial Service's Speakers Program, which provides associations with expert speakers on various industry topics for annual meetings, conferences, and round tables.

TPCC AGENCY INITIATIVES TO IMPROVE ACCESS TO EXPORT ASSISTANCE

The Federal Government provides a wide range of trade education, market research, match-making, risk management, and problem-solving services that exporters need. Changes in technology, U.S. industry, and foreign markets dictate that government must keep pace with the changing needs of exporters. Our ability to do so is as important to the individual potential exporter as to our strategic partners, if we are to hold up our end of the partnership. It is important, therefore, for government to continuously demonstrate improvements in access to its services. Succeeding in this task is doubly important if we hope to broaden and deepen the base of exporters. There are several recent examples of the TPCC agencies working to make services more relevant and accessible, especially for small companies and new exporters who need help most. The TPCC agencies will work to fully implement and maximize the potential of these initiatives.

U.S. Department of Commerce Initiatives

Streamlined User Fee Schedule: In May 2008, the Commercial Service implemented a new user fee schedule to improve customer service and enable more U.S. companies—especially small and medium-sized firms—to leverage the Commercial Service's global network of trade experts. Under the new fee structure, customers will now pay the same fees worldwide for a Commercial Service standard service, no matter where they do business. For instance, the Gold Key Matchmaking Service will now be $700 for SMEs across all markets worldwide. The new schedule maintains low fees for small and medium-sized companies, improving access to Commercial Service export assistance for those that most need it. Further, the new user fee schedule provides an incentive for qualifying new-to-export companies to try Commercial Service services for the first time: up to a 50 percent discount for the Commercial Service Gold Key Service, International Company Profile, International Partner Search, or Featured U.S. Exporter service. The goal is to encourage new-to-export SMEs to try our services for the first time. A full description of the U.S. Commercial Service new user fee schedule is located at www.export.gov.

Featured U.S. Exporter Service (FUSE): The Commercial Service's FUSE program leverages the power of the Internet and the Commercial Service's overseas network of physical offices to provide affordable local promotion worldwide. FUSE has been expanded to more than 60 markets worldwide, and to more than 15 different languages. FUSE is an online directory of U.S. products and services featured on Commercial Service Web sites around the world. It gives companies an opportunity to reach prospects in the local language of the target market. For a low annual subscription rate, a company's profile is featured, in English or the local language, in the FUSE directory of the market(s) in which the company wants to do business. Local buyers, distributors, and agents see that company's profile and send inquiries to the Commercial Service. After confirming the foreign company's viability, purchasing interest, and contact details, the sales lead is sent on to the U.S. company.

Online Pay: Online payment for Commercial Service services was launched in January 2008 to enhance the customer experience. Online Pay lets prospective clients express interest in a standard or customized service, receive a statement of work for the proposed service, and pay online using a credit card. These changes improve the Commercial Service's consistency of service delivery and management of client relationships.

Trade Finance Guide: In 2007, the International Trade Administration's Office of Finance issued the first edition of the *Trade Finance Guide: A Quick Reference for U.S. Exporters.* With the guide in high demand by the exporting community, a second edition was published in April 2008. The guide is targeted to SMEs, with concise, two-page chapters that offer the basics of numerous financing techniques and the specific situations for considering each. The latest edition includes a chapter on foreign exchange risk management as well as updates to all of the other chapters. The guide was created in partnership with the Association of Executives in Finance, Credit, and International Business (FCIB) and with the cooperation of SBA, Ex-Im Bank, and various other private trade associations. It is available from the Trade Information Center (1-800-USA-TRAD(E)) and U.S. Export Assistance Centers nationwide or in PDF format at www.ita.doc.gov/media/Publications/abstract/trade_finance_guide2008desc.html.

Safe Harbor Certification Mark: The free flow of data across borders is critical to trade. In June 2008, the Department of Commerce issued a certification mark for the U.S.-European Union (EU) Safe Harbor Framework. The Safe Harbor Framework first established in 2000 ensures uninterrupted transfers of personal information worth billions of dollars in trade between the EU and the United States. The new certification mark may be used by companies on their Web sites to signify their compliance with the provisions of the Safe Harbor Framework. As the program has grown, and achieved global recognition as one of the best ways to meet the requirements of the EU's Data Protection Directive, U.S. companies asked for a means to illustrate their participation in and compliance with the Safe Harbor Framework. EU Data Protection officials have also noted their support for the certification mark. Nearly 1,500 U.S. companies participate in the Safe Harbor. The program is managed by ITA's Manufacturing and Services unit.

Export Controls Online Training: The Department of Commerce's Bureau of Industry and Security (BIS) has launched a new online training room that offers an introductory series of easy-to-use training modules covering the materials from the Essentials of Export Controls seminars currently offered around the country. This free service saves exporters—particularly small and medium-sized enterprises—both time and money, and provides flexibility to those who would like to learn more about export regulations. "The BIS Online Training Room is a convenient, easy-to-use, and valuable tool for exporters, particularly small and medium-sized enterprises," says Mario Mancuso, Under Secretary of Commerce for Industry and Security. "The new modules help exporters understand and comply with our Regulations, allowing them to take advantage of exciting global trading opportunities."

OPIC Expanding Horizon Workshops

Building on the success of a series of workshops for minority and woman-owned businesses in 2006 and early 2007, OPIC launched a new series in September 2007, providing hundreds of businesses in Newark, Houston, and San Francisco an opportunity to learn how products and services offered by OPIC and other government agencies can help them expand into emerging markets overseas. The workshops are called "Expanding Horizons," and are held in cooperation with the U.S. Department of Commerce's Minority Business Development Agency and the National Women's Business Council. Previous workshops were held in Atlanta, Chicago, Los Angeles, and Miami. OPIC established the workshops out of awareness that minority and woman-owned businesses face unique challenges in their efforts to gain entry to the global marketplace—lack of knowledge about government programs available to support overseas investment; scarcity of capital to pursue opportunities abroad; and concern over political risks in emerging markets—that have prevented them from expanding overseas.

Ex-Im Bank's Expanded Online Services

Ex-Im Bank has continued to enhance its "Ex-Im Online" system, with the goal of making it faster and easier for program users to work with Ex-Im Bank. Ex-Im Online is an interactive, Web-based process that allows exporters, brokers, and financial institutions to transact with Ex-Im Bank electronically. Via Ex-Im Online, users can apply for Ex-Im Bank support, monitor the status of an application, view and accept quotes, report shipments, obtain buyer approvals, and request policy amendments. The transaction types now available in Ex-Im Bank Online are short-term single-buyer insurance, short-term multi-buyer insurance, financial institution buyer credit insurance, letter of credit insurance for banks, medium-term insurance, medium-term loan guarantees, and medium-term finance lease guarantees. Users can access the Ex-Im Online system at www.exim.gov/news/exim_online_spl.cfm.

U.S. Department of Agriculture Electronic Leads

In April 2008, FAS, the National Association of State Departments of Agriculture, and New Media Solutions, Inc. released a new Web-based, "back-office" IT system that allows FAS field offices to disseminate agricultural trade leads originating from foreign buyers directly to key contacts at State Departments of Agriculture and SRTGs for export opportunity review. The system improves the quality and targeting of business opportunities to U.S. suppliers and the ability to track the overall success of each export opportunity generated through the system.

Free Trade Agreements

"On trade, we must trust American workers to compete with anyone in the world and empower them by opening up new markets overseas. Today, our economic growth increasingly depends on our ability to sell American goods and crops and services all over the world. So we're working to break down barriers to trade and investment wherever we can. We're working for a successful Doha Round of trade talks, and we must complete a good agreement this year. At the same time, we're pursuing opportunities to open up new markets by passing free trade agreements."

—President George W. Bush, State of the Union Address, January 28, 2008

An important driver of U.S. exports is the reduction of trade barriers through multilateral, regional, and bilateral trade agreements. Several decades of successful multilateral negotiations under the auspices of the General Agreement on Tariffs and Trade (1947) and now the World Trade Organization (WTO), as well as successful regional trade agreements such as the North American Free Trade Agreement (NAFTA), have helped to make the United States the world's largest exporter of goods and services today. The benefits of trade have accrued to our businesses, workers, families, communities, and trading partners. The United States' top trade priority in 2008 is realizing an agreement on modalities that leads to a successful conclusion to the Doha Round.[1] Achieving substantial market opening for goods and services would make our economy more competitive and more productive. Further, only through such an outcome will the development promise of Doha be met, by creating new economic opportunities worldwide.

The multilateral WTO agreements and NAFTA collectively result in a boost of $1,300 to $2,000 in the annual income of the average American family of four.[2] The United States today has stronger economic growth, higher manufacturing output, and lower unemployment because of these agreements.

The U.S. Government's consistent support of free and fair trade has positioned U.S. companies to take full advantage of rapid foreign economic growth and improved terms of trade.

1   "Doha Round" refers to the multilateral trade negotiations launched in Doha, Qatar, in November 2001, known as the Doha Development Agenda (DDA or Doha Round). The DDA is the ninth successive round of multilateral trade negotiations to be carried out since the end of World War II.

2   James Langenfeld and James Nieberding, "The Benefits of Free Trade to U.S. Consumers: Quantitative Confirmation of Theoretical Expectation," *Business Economics* 40, No. 3 (July, 2005).

*Note: World GDP excludes
the United States. GDP
figures on a purchasing-
power parity basis. Export
figures are for total U.S.
merchandise exports.
FTA Countries include all
countries with free trade
agreements in force with the
United States (Australia,
Bahrain, Canada, Chile,
the Dominican Republic,
El Salvador, Guatemala,
Honduras, Israel, Jordan,
Mexico, Morocco, Nicaragua
and Singapore).*

Source: International Monetary Fund,
World Economic Outlook, Database
(October 2007); U.S. Department of
Commerce, Bureau of the Census,
Foreign Trade Division.

CHART 10

U.S. FREE TRADE AGREEMENT PARTNERS IN THE GLOBAL ECONOMY

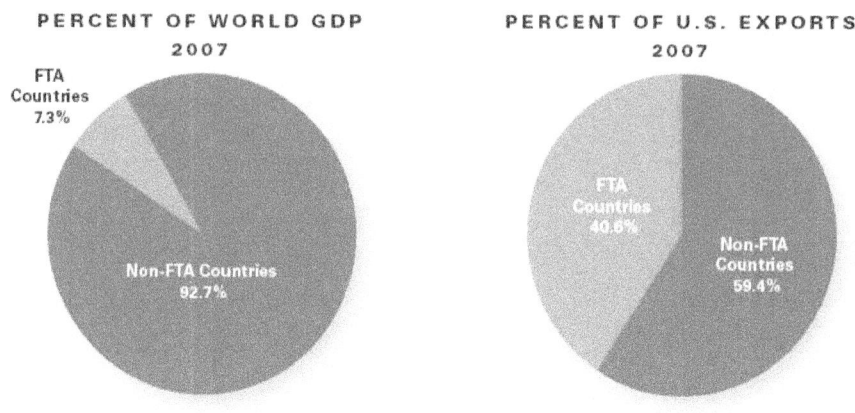

Steady bipartisan leadership in approving trade agreements has helped U.S. exports to grow faster than general economic growth for most of the past 20 years. As the United States experiences economic adjustment at home, it is more important than ever for our businesses, farmers, and workers that one of the critical legs of our economy —exports—not be knocked out from under them. The successful conclusion of the Doha Development Agenda negotiations, as well as Congressional approval of free trade agreements (FTAs) with Colombia, Panama, and South Korea, will ensure that exports continue to support and sustain U.S. economic growth and prosperity. The Bush Administration also continues to lay the groundwork for future agreements in key markets. The United States hopes to reengage Thailand on FTA talks when both sides are ready and to make further significant progress toward conclusion of an FTA with Malaysia. On a regional basis, the Administration continues to promote free and open trade and investment, and increased regional economic integration within the Asia Pacific Economic Cooperation forum (APEC)[3], including by intensively exploring the prospect of a Free Trade Area of the Asia Pacific (FTAAP).

U.S. FTA RECORD OF SUCCESS

Access to the markets of U.S. FTA partners has contributed to overall U.S. export success. Exports in 2007 to our 14 FTA partners with agreements in force accounted for nearly one-quarter of the growth of U.S. goods exports over 2006. In 2007, U.S. combined exports to our 14 FTA partners were much greater than those partners' relative share of the global economy. While composing just 7.3 percent of global GDP (excluding the United States), those FTA countries accounted for 40.6 percent of U.S. exports (*Chart 10*).

Trade also tends to be more balanced with our FTA trading partners. Our combined trade deficit with FTA partner countries is smaller than with non-FTA countries. In 2007, 16 percent of our overall trade deficit resulted from trade with FTA trading partners, compared to 84 percent attributed to trade with non-FTA trading partners (*Chart 11*). In the absence of

---

3   APEC member economies: Australia, Brunei, Canada, Chile, China, Hong Kong, China, Indonesia, Japan, Korea, Malaysia, Mexico, New Zealand, Papua New Guinea, Peru, the Philippines, Russia, Singapore, the United States, Taiwan, Thailand, and Vietnam.

CHART 11

FTAs AND THE TRADE BALANCE, 2007

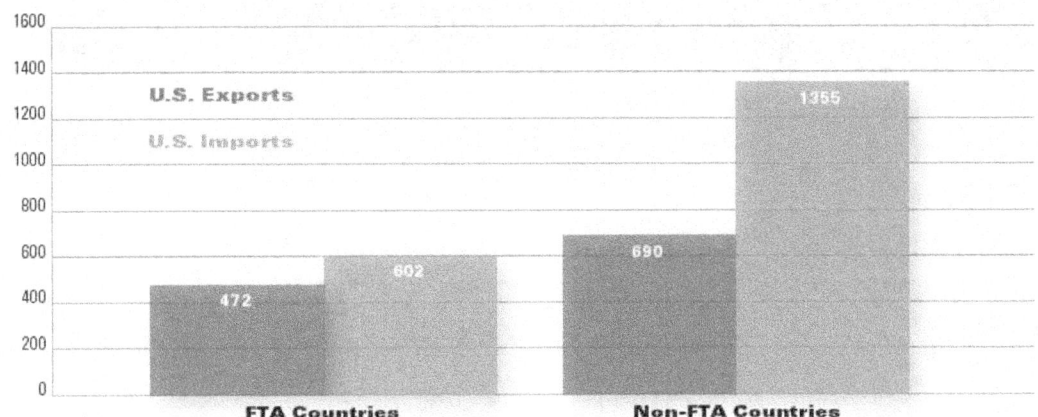

Notes: Figures include all
countries with free trade
agreements in force with
the United States (Australia,
Bahrain, Canada, Chile,
the Dominican Republic,
El Salvador, Guatemala,
Honduras, Israel, Jordan,
Mexico, Morocco, Nicaragua
and Singapore). Export
figures are for Total Exports
on a Free Alongside Ship
basis. Import figures are
the Customs value of U.S.
General Imports.

Source: U.S. Department of Commerce,
Bureau of the Census, Foreign Trade
Division.

an FTA, U.S. goods exporters typically face significantly higher trade barriers than foreign companies face exporting to the United States. This is especially true in developing countries, which generally maintain much higher import duties than the United States. Eliminating duties and non-tariff barriers can have a significant effect on trade. In 2005, for example, the U.S. trade deficit with the Dominican Republic-Central America-United States Free Trade Agreement (CAFTA-DR) countries was $1.2 billion. By 2007, this deficit had become a U.S. surplus with the CAFTA-DR countries of $3.7 billion.

In 2006, FTAs were implemented with the following six trading partners: Bahrain, El Salvador, Guatemala, Honduras, Morocco, and Nicaragua. In 2007, CAFTA-DR entered into force with the Dominican Republic, and in 2008, we expect that this Agreement will enter into force for Costa Rica. We also expect that our FTA with Oman will enter into force in 2008. Congress has already approved the United States-Peru Trade Promotion Agreement. This agreement—as well as the agreements with Colombia, Panama, and South Korea, when they are approved and enter into force—will continue to fuel growth as tariff and non-tariff barriers are phased out as each agreement is implemented.

Importance of FTAs to Small Companies

FTAs are especially important for small and medium-sized enterprises (SMEs), which benefit most from reductions in tariff rates and regulatory red tape, as well as from general improvements in the commercial environment and business transparency. In 2006 (latest available data), over 90 percent of U.S. companies exporting to Canada, Mexico, and Australia were SMEs. Seventy percent or more of U.S. companies exporting to all other FTA partner countries were SMEs. SMEs also account for an above-average share (above 29 percent) of U.S. exports in eight of the 14 FTA partner countries (*Table 2*).

TABLE 2

U.S. SME EXPORTS TO FTA TRADING PARTNERS, 2006

Country	SME Export Value ($ millions)	SME Share of Total Exports (percent)
Australia	4,249	27.3
Bahrain	122	35.6
Canada	134	20.8
Chile	674	28.4
Dominican Republic	731	56.0
El Salvador	895	47.5
Guatemala	1,500	47.5
Honduras	1,249	37.7
Israel	3,384	42.3
Jordan	231	44.9
Mexico	32,496	27.5
Morocco	200	23.7
Nicaragua	440	64.6
Singapore	4,304	19.1

Source: U.S. Department of Commerce, Exporter Database.

FTAs Since 2001

U.S. goods exports to the 11 FTA countries with which agreements entered into force since 2001 are growing faster than exports to the rest of the world. Specifically, U.S. goods exports to the 11 FTA countries have increased 71 percent since 2001, versus 59 percent for exports to the rest of the world over that same time period.

Jordan: The United States-Jordan FTA entered into force on December 17, 2001. Since 2001, U.S. merchandise exports to Jordan have increased 153 percent, or by $517 million, reaching $856 million in 2007. Of the top exporting sectors by value, the fastest export growth over this period occurred in the vehicles (1,500 percent), aircraft (679 percent), and aluminum (581 percent) sectors.

Chile: The United States-Chile FTA entered into force January 1, 2004. Since 2003, U.S. merchandise exports to Chile have increased 206 percent, or by $5.6 billion, reaching $8.3 billion in 2007. Of the top exporting sectors by value, the fastest export growth over this period occurred in the mineral fuels (2,510 percent), aircraft (1,986 percent), and cereals (349 percent) sectors.

Singapore: The United States-Singapore FTA entered into force January 1, 2004. Since 2003, U.S. merchandise exports to Singapore have increased 59 percent, or by $9.7 billion, reaching $26.3 billion in 2007. This growth in U.S. exports has caused the U.S. trade balance with Singapore to improve from a $1.4 billion surplus in 2003 to a $7.9 billion surplus in 2007. Of the top exporting sectors by value, the fastest export growth over this period occurred in the mineral fuels (240 percent), organic chemicals (110 percent), and iron and steel articles (110 percent) sectors.

Australia: The United States-Australia FTA entered into force January 1, 2005. Since 2004, U.S. merchandise exports to Australia have increased 35 percent, or by $5.0 billion, reaching $19.2 billion in 2007. This growth in U.S. exports has caused the U.S. trade balance with Australia to improve from a $6.7 billion surplus in 2004 to a $10.6 billion surplus in 2007. Of the top exporting sectors by value, the fastest export growth over this period occurred in the railway/traffic signal (130 percent), plastics (62 percent), and pharmaceuticals (50 percent) sectors.

Morocco: The United States-Morocco FTA entered into force January 1, 2006. Since 2005, U.S. merchandise exports to Morocco have increased 156 percent, or $818 million, reaching $1.3 billion in 2007. This growth in U.S. exports has caused the U.S. trade balance with Morocco to improve from a $79 million surplus in 2005 to a $733 million surplus in 2007. Of the top exporting sectors by value, some of the fastest export growth over this period occurred in the plastics (1,353 percent), mineral fuels (1,363 percent), and cereals (399 percent) sectors.

El Salvador: The CAFTA-DR agreement entered into force between the United States and El Salvador on March 1, 2006. Since 2005, U.S. merchandise exports to El Salvador have increased 25 percent, or by $459 million, reaching $2.3 billion in 2007. Of the top exporting sectors by value, the fastest export growth over this period occurred in the mineral fuels (300 percent), cotton yarns/fabric (74 percent), and electrical machinery/equipment (64 percent) sectors.

Nicaragua: The CAFTA-DR agreement entered into force between the United States and Nicaragua on April 1, 2006. Since 2005, U.S. merchandise exports to Nicaragua have increased 42 percent, or by $265 million, reaching $890 million in 2007. Of the top exporting sectors by value, the fastest export growth over this period occurred in the mineral fuels (417 percent), knitted/crocheted fabric (91 percent), and animal or vegetable oils (80 percent) sectors.

Honduras: The CAFTA-DR agreement entered into force between the United States and Honduras on April 1, 2006. Since 2005, U.S. merchandise exports to Honduras have increased 37 percent, or by $1.2 billion, reaching $4.5 billion in 2007. Of the top exporting sectors by value, the fastest export growth over this period occurred in the mineral fuels (155 percent), electrical machinery/equipment (69 percent), and manmade fibers (56 percent) sectors.

Guatemala: The CAFTA-DR agreement entered into force between the United States and Guatemala on July 1, 2006. Since 2005, U.S. merchandise exports to Guatemala have increased 43 percent, or by $1.2 billion, reaching $4.1 billion in 2007. Of the top exporting sectors by value, the fastest export growth over this period occurred in the mineral fuels (89 percent), cereals (86 percent), and plastics (75 percent) sectors.

Bahrain: The United States-Bahrain FTA entered into force on August 1, 2006. Since 2005, U.S. merchandise exports to Bahrain have increased 69 percent, or by $241 million, reaching $591 million in 2007. Of the top exporting sectors by value, the fastest export growth over this period occurred in the mineral fuels (2,152 percent), iron and steel articles (1,017 percent), and precious stones and metals (350 percent) sectors.

Dominican Republic: The CAFTA-DR agreement entered into force between the United States and the Dominican Republic on March 1, 2007. Since 2006, U.S. merchandise exports to the Dominican Republic have increased 14 percent, or by $734 million, reaching $6.1 billion in 2007. Of the top exporting sectors by value, the fastest export growth over this period

"Peru has a burgeoning transportation sector, and an FTA will enable us to increase our sales and number of distributors, allowing us to better compete with firms from Brazil, Chile, and Venezuela who already benefit from reduced barriers through free trade with Peru."
—Orlando Serna, Export Sales Manager for Latin America

Midwest Truck & Auto Parts, Inc. specializes in heavy-duty truck hardware such as gears, axle bearings, and engine parts. With help from the Commercial Service in nearby Libertyville, Illinois and in Peru, the Andean country has become a major market for the company. Mr. Serna sees even more potential with a Peru FTA. With the help of the Commercial Service, Midwest is also exporting to Russia, Honduras, Jamaica, Mexico, and the United Arab Emirates.

Photo: Orlando Serna, of Midwest Truck & Auto Parts, in the company's warehouse in Chicago.

occurred in the optical/medical instruments (62 percent), electrical machinery/equipment (44 percent), and vehicles (38 percent) sectors.

Congressionally Approved Agreements Awaiting Entry into Force

Peru: The United States and Peru signed the United States-Peru Trade Promotion Agreement (U.S.-Peru TPA) on April 12, 2006 and a protocol of amendment on June 24, 2007. The Peruvian Congress ratified the agreement in June 2006 and the protocol of amendment in June 2007. After overwhelming House and Senate votes on legislation approving the agreement, President Bush signed the U.S.-Peru TPA Implementation Act on December 14, 2007. Since the Andean Trade Preference Act was first enacted in 1991, Peru has enjoyed duty-free access to the U.S. market. The U.S.-Peru TPA will give U.S. exporters equivalent access to the Peruvian market. In 2007, U.S.-Peru trade totaled over $9.4 billion dollars. When the agreement enters into force, 80 percent of U.S. exports of consumer and industrial goods to Peru will enter duty-free immediately, with remaining tariffs phased out over 10 years. Additionally, nearly 90 percent of current agricultural trade will receive duty-free treatment, and tariffs on other agricultural products will be eliminated over time, most within five to 15 years.

Costa Rica: The CAFTA-DR is now in force for all signatories to the agreement except Costa Rica. The people of Costa Rica approved the CAFTA-DR in a national referendum in October 2007. Entry into force is pending adoption of necessary implementing legislation and regulations by Costa Rica.

Oman: The United States signed a free trade agreement with Oman on January 19, 2006. President Bush signed legislation approving the agreement on September 26, 2006, following Congressional action. Oman continues to work on its implementing legislation. In 2007, U.S. goods exported to Oman totaled $1.1 billion.

FTAs Requiring Congressional Approval

As a group, pending FTAs with Colombia, Panama, and South Korea represent access for U.S. companies to nearly 100 million customers. These agreements also promote America's strategic and other interests.

Colombia: The Bush Administration sent legislation regarding the United States-Colombia Trade Promotion Agreement to Congress for approval on April 8, 2008; Congress has not yet considered the legislation. Colombia is our fourth-largest trading partner in Latin America and is the largest market for U.S. agriculture exports in South and Central America, as well as in the Caribbean. Over 90 percent of U.S. imports from Colombia now enter our country duty-free. Currently, no U.S. agricultural exports enjoy duty-free entry into the Colombian market. In fact, U.S. exports to Colombia face duties as high as 35 percent in the case of industrial and consumer goods, and much higher for many agricultural products. Under the agreement, all of Colombia's tariffs would go to zero. Upon entry into force, the agreement will immediately eliminate tariffs on more than 80 percent of American exports of industrial and consumer goods, and on more than half of U.S. agricultural exports. In addition, the agreement would allow trade in remanufactured products and eliminate other significant barriers to U.S. exports, such as Colombia's price bands on agricultural products. U.S. Congressional approval and entry into force of the Colombia free trade agreement will create favorable conditions and incentives to support sustained real growth, create more jobs, and attract new investment in Colombia. This agreement also will help bolster the Government of Colombia's policies promoting greater openness, transparency, and accountability, and further strengthen Colombia's democratic institutions and the rule of law.

USTDA COUNTRY OF THE YEAR AWARD TO COLOMBIA

In March 2008, the U.S. Trade and Development Agency (USTDA) presented the agency's 2007 Country of the Year award to Colombia, which was accepted by Colombian President Álvaro Uribe Vélez, reflecting the success of its program in advancing mutual economic benefits and U.S. policy priorities. Colombia worked with USTDA on the implementation of a broad program that achieved significant measurable successes. For example, the agency supported a technical assistance program with the Port of Cartagena on chain-of-custody security, contributing to the Port's compliance certification in 2007 by U.S. Customs and Border Protection under the Container Security Initiative. USTDA funded two separate studies and an orientation visit to the United States for senior Ecopetrol officials in conjunction with plans for a refinery expansion in Cartagena. An $80 million engineering, procurement, and construction contract has been awarded to Chicago Bridge and Iron of Chicago, Illinois. USTDA has also funded other activities to further the development of new natural gas and petroleum resources and expanded refining capacity in Colombia. USTDA is also working to diversify Colombia's energy supply and promote the development of clean energy resources. USTDA is assisting ISAGEN S.A. E.S.P. with its plans for a 50 megawatt geothermal power plant and the conversion of AeroCivil's power supply for its air traffic control and weather monitoring facilities in remote areas.

Photo: Then USTDA Acting Director Leocadia Zak presenting award to Colombian President Álvaro Uribe Vélez.

"We see clear benefits from a Colombia FTA, because any time you can knock down barriers and see taxes reduced, that makes us more competitive. Our worldwide exports have contributed significantly to the growth of Hytrol and help support manufacturing jobs here in Arkansas."

—Dan Fischbacher, Director of International Operations

Hytrol Conveyor Company of Jonesboro, Arkansas, is a manufacturer of conveying equipment used for assembly lines and other industrial operations. With help from the Commercial Service in Arkansas and Colombia, and the Ex-Im Bank, the firm is expanding its distribution network in South America. Mr. Dan Fischbacher, Director of International Operations, says Colombia is becoming an increasingly attractive market because of its pro-business environment and large demand for packaging, distribution, and pallet handling. The company has been a client of the Little Rock Export Assistance Center since 1983.

Photo: Hytrol conveying equipment in action.

Panama: In 2007, Panama and the United States exchanged around $4 billion worth of goods—nearly two times more than just four years ago. Panama is one of the fastest-growing economies in Central America, with a growth rate of more than eight percent last year. The United States and Panama signed the United States-Panama Trade Promotion Agreement (U.S.-Panama TPA) on June 28, 2007. When this agreement enters into force, duties on nearly 88 percent of U.S. consumer and industrial exports to Panama and on more than 60 percent of U.S. agricultural products will be eliminated immediately. The agreement will create opportunities for U.S. businesses to participate in the Panama Canal expansion project. It will also provide new market access for U.S. service suppliers, including in Panama's key financial services sector.

South Korea: The United States-Korea Free Trade Agreement (KORUS FTA) is the most commercially significant bilateral free trade agreement the United States has concluded in the past 15 years. South Korea is already our seventh-largest goods trading partner, with $82 billion in bilateral trade in 2007. The KORUS FTA will open a country with a $1 trillion GDP and a growing market of 49 million consumers to a full range of U.S. goods and services, from autos to telecommunications and financial services. The U.S. International Trade Commission estimates the reduction of Korean tariffs and tariff-rate quota provisions on goods market access alone would add $10-12 billion to annual U.S. GDP, meaning an increase of better-paying jobs for American workers. Under the KORUS FTA, Korea and the United States will eliminate tariffs on nearly 95 percent of bilateral trade in consumer and industrial products within three years, and almost two-thirds of U.S. agriculture exports to Korea will become duty-free immediately. The free trade agreement will also address a range of non-tariff barriers and increase transparency in Korea's regulatory processes. In addition, the KORUS FTA will add an important new economic element to the close strategic partnership that the United States has maintained with South Korea on the Korean Peninsula for over 60 years.

RheoSense is a Korean-American-owned start-up company, and a manufacturer of smart sensor devices for measurements of plastics, polymers, or other materials essential for process and quality control. Dr. Seong-Gi Baek first contacted the Commercial Service's U.S. Export Assistance Center in Oakland, California, in early 2005 seeking help with an order from Seoul University. After contacting the Commercial Service office in Seoul, the U.S. Export Assistance Center in Oakland determined that there were no tariffs and no Korean Customs Services approvals needed. As a result, RheoSense was able to complete a major export sale to this new buyer, Seoul University. Dr. Baek continues to expand his sales to South Korea and has also entered the Swiss and United Kingdom markets with the assistance of the Commercial Service.

Photo: Dr. Seong-Gi Baek, President/CEO and founder of RheoSense, demonstrates his smart sensor devices to Trade Specialist Rod Hirsch at the Oakland U.S. Export Assistance Center.

TPCC AGENCY INITIATIVES

A continuing priority of the export promotion agencies is sustained follow-up in FTA markets. Especially given the importance of these markets to smaller companies, a major goal is to raise U.S. business awareness of new market access and of tools available to enter these markets.

Geographically Cross-Cutting Initiatives

Commercial Service "Trade Americas—FTA Roadshow": During World Trade Month in May 2008, the Trade Americas Team of the Commercial Service conducted a nationwide series of business seminars on how to leverage trade agreements to increase export sales. During these seminars, companies met with Commercial Service Officers from U.S. embassies in FTA partner countries, Washington trade policy experts, and other public and private-sector export services providers. Roadshow events were held in Charlotte, North Carolina; Trenton, New Jersey; Pittsburgh, Pennsylvania; St. Louis, Missouri; San Jose, California; Seattle, Washington; and Salt Lake City, Utah. Events reached more than 350 small to medium-sized companies.

Millennium Challenge Corporation (MCC) Support in FTA Partner Countries: The MCC is committed to development, poverty reduction, and economic growth in the Americas, including five-year compacts with three CAFTA-DR trading partners—El Salvador, Honduras, and Nicaragua—totaling more than $850 million. In addition, in early 2008, the MCC Board approved Peru's $35.6 million Threshold Program. In August 2007, Morocco and the MCC signed a $697.5 million grant to spur economic growth and increase employment opportunities, including a fruit tree productivity project and a small-scale fisheries project.

USDA/FAS Market Access Activities: FAS' market access activities include a country and/or regional approach to maximizing trade opportunities for U.S. agricultural exporters. It provides market intelligence, in-country resolution of disruptions or potential disruptions to U.S. shipments, and regular contacts with foreign government agricultural and trade officials.

Central America and the Caribbean

OPIC Access to Opportunity in Central America and the Caribbean Conference: In May 2007, OPIC hosted the Access to Opportunity Conference in El Salvador to identify investment opportunities in the region for U.S. companies, and to cap off an intensive two-year OPIC focus on the region. Almost 300 participants from 15 countries attended the three-day conference. "Enabling U.S. companies to familiarize themselves with these markets, and regional companies to access new sources of capital, is the goal of this conference," said OPIC President and CEO Robert Mosbacher, Jr. Since becoming OPIC President and CEO in late 2005, Mosbacher has visited the Central America/Caribbean region five times, including a visit to announce $332 million in new OPIC-supported U.S. investment in Central America, primarily in the housing and microfinance sectors.

USTDA CAFTA-DR Trade Integration Initiative: USTDA continues to expand activity under the CAFTA-DR Initiative launched in 2005 to support priority projects in Central America that further the benefits of increased trade, regional connectivity and economic growth under CAFTA-DR. To date, USTDA has invested over $8 million under the Initiative in support of the region's National Trade Capacity Building Strategies. Recent activity includes:

El Salvador: In April 2008, USTDA awarded two grants totaling $1.1 million in El Salvador that complement MCC infrastructure investments. The goal is to promote the establishment of the necessary infrastructure and capacity for private sector trade and investment to serve as a catalyst for growth in El Salvador's Northern Zone. The grants complement the MCC's anti-poverty Compact in El Salvador. By coordinating their efforts, USTDA and the MCC seek to increase the effectiveness of their individual programs.

Costa Rica: In September 2007, USTDA awarded two grants supporting development of Costa Rica's electric power infrastructure. The grants to the Coast Rican Institute of Electricity, the state-owned electricity and telecommunications company, will fund the geotechnical and financial components of a larger study of the proposed El Diquis hydroelectric power project.

Guatemala: In August 2007, USTDA awarded a grant to support the development of Guatemala's information and communications infrastructure. This grant to the Guatemalan Superintendent of Tax Administration will support technical assistance in the improvement of the Customs Transit Control System.

Secretarial Business Development Mission to Central America and the Dominican Republic: Secretary of Commerce Carlos M. Gutierrez led a senior-level U.S. business delegation to Costa Rica and the Dominican Republic from September 28–October 2, 2008, to promote U.S. exports and investment in the leading industry sectors in Central America and the Dominican Republic, and to highlight regional opportunities for U.S. businesses arising under the CAFTA-DR agreement. In addition to helping U.S. firms increase their exports and participation in major projects in the CAFTA-DR countries, the mission provided a platform for policy and commercial issues—including transparency, rule of law, financial reform and intellectual-property rights protection—that U.S. companies face in these markets. Representatives of OPIC, USTDA, and Ex-Im Bank participated.

The Middle East and North Africa

USTDA Initiatives in the MENA Region: In 2007, USTDA invested more than $3.7 million in activities throughout the Middle East and North Africa (MENA) region. In the past year, projects in FTA partner countries Jordan and Morocco focused on the wastewater and solid waste treatment sector.

Morocco: In September 2007, USTDA awarded a grant to the Office of Potable Water to help Morocco identify viable solutions for wastewater treatment throughout the country. The grant funds early investment analysis on the construction of a proposed industrial wastewater treatment system in the city of Berrechid.

Jordan: Also in September 2007, USTDA expanded its support of wastewater and solid waste treatment in Jordan to more than $1.1 million. The award to the Jordanian Ministry of Environment funds a study that will recommend a solution to reduce the current level of pollution in the Zarqa River Basin and protect biodiversity and public health.

North America

USDA—endorsed Trade Shows in Canada and Mexico: In 2007, the U.S. Department of Agriculture supported U.S. participation in six major trade shows in Canada and Mexico to promote exports of U.S. agricultural goods, including the Canadian Restaurant and Foodservices Association and the SIAL Montreal shows in Canada; and the Antad, Alimentaria Mexico, Exphotel, and Abastur shows in Mexico. During SIAL Montreal, for example, U.S. companies were invited to join the official USDA-endorsed USA Pavilion (pictured below), with market-

Thirty-five companies participated in the USA Pavilion at SIAL Montreal 2007. These companies introduced 298 new products, had 608 serious contacts, and estimated 12-month projected sales of $1.3 million as a result of the event.

ing support from USDA's Office of Agricultural Affairs in Ottawa, including local promotion to importers, on-site market briefing, and on-going market assistance during the show. USDA also regularly supports shows in the FTA partner countries of Australia and Morocco.

Commercial Service United States-Mexico Border Initiative: The United States provides an estimated 47 percent of all inputs to the *maquiladoras* (export manufacturing plants), valued conservatively at $41 billion in U.S. exports. As the U.S. and Mexican economies experience further integration, the more than 2,800 such plants throughout Mexico—of which 60 percent are located along the border with the United States—will have an ongoing need to source quality inputs, equipment, and services from U.S. industry. To better help U.S. businesses tap sales opportunities offered by the *maquiladoras*, the Commercial Service launched the Border Trade Initiative (BTI). The BTI extends the strong trade promotion programs that already exist throughout Mexico and on the border in Tijuana, to include the significant manufacturing clusters that have been underserved by the Commercial Service in the Mexican states bordering Arizona, New Mexico, and Texas. The BTI is being gradually implemented throughout the border region in 2008, and will build on the success of the Tijuana office in offering matchmaking services, hands-on border region programs, special events, market research, and other tools to help U.S. businesses be successful in accessing this important market. The Commercial Service in Mexico maintains a schedule of upcoming events including seminars and trade shows throughout 2008.[4]

Commerce-USTDA—The United States and Mexico: Building Partnerships in Infrastructure Conference: On February 26–28, 2008, USTDA and the Commercial Service co-sponsored the Conference in Mexico City. Over 400 participants joined the event, designed to promote U.S.-Mexican business ventures in ports, aviation, energy, and the environment. U.S. Ambassador to Mexico Antonio Garza, U.S. Secretary of Commerce Carlos M. Gutierrez, then USTDA Acting Director Leocadia Zak, and several senior cabinet members of the Mexican government joined the plenary session attended by U.S. and Mexican company representatives. Ex-Im Bank Vice Chair Linda Conlin gave remarks at the Finance Plenary, and FedEx Mexico sponsored a major networking event. During the Conference, USTDA signed $1.7 million in grants for infrastructure projects in support of Mexico's National Infrastructure Program objectives, which include studies on expanding Puebla International Airport, Queretaro International Airport, and San Luis Potosi International Airport; studies on a proposed municipal water desalination facility in the state of Sonora; and, technical assistance for strengthening environmental management at power plants, substations, and power transmission and distribution facilities.

4 www.buyusa.gov/mexico/en/border_trade_initiative.html

"NAFTA has reduced the costs of selling to Mexico, including duties, thereby making us even more competitive. We've also seen a great reduction in paperwork that has contributed to our cost savings."
—Michele LaNoue, owner/CEO

Headworks Inc. is a woman-owned small business that specializes in wastewater treatment technology that screens out solid wastes at water treatment plants. With bilingual representation and help from the Commercial Service in Houston and Mexico City, Headworks recently made major new-to-market sales to Mexico. Headworks CEO LaNoue says Mexico's increased emphasis on environmental quality is opening new doors of opportunity for pollution control technologies. The firm's overall export sales, including those to Mexico, have enabled her company to grow and support new jobs at its Houston headquarters. LaNoue also serves as the Houston District Export Council's Chairperson.

Priority Markets

The Federal Government focuses trade promotion resources on FTA partner countries, given the opportunities created by new market access and an improving business environment. However, the TPCC also identifies priority markets each year based on global trends and sheer commercial potential for U.S. exports. These spotlight markets are large and have high rates of growth. But typically they are also more difficult for U.S. companies to navigate. As such, these countries are where U.S. Government assistance can play a significant role in helping U.S. companies succeed. This year, priority markets fitting this description are China, India, Brazil, and Russia. While emerging and developing markets as a whole continue to grow at an impressive rate, these four countries account for almost one-half of the growth in global activity over the past five years.[1] As growth in the advanced economies slows in the face of financial turmoil, these countries are forecast to continue growing at a rate of 5 to 10 percent in 2008.

Reasons for strong growth in these markets range from increased integration into the global economy to strong commodity exports. Emerging markets are also credited with improved management of macroeconomic and fiscal policy, and with productivity gains and economic diversification. Progress on these fronts has, in turn, fueled more stable economic growth, growing domestic consumption, and demand for imports across many sectors.

CROSSCUTTING FOCUS ON INFRASTRUCTURE

As countries work to enable and sustain this growth and integrate with the global economy, there has been an across-the-board increase in critical infrastructure needs and spending. As countries industrialize, an increasing percentage of the population is migrating to urban centers, creating additional demand for major electricity, water, and transportation system improvements. According to a Booz Allen Hamilton study,[2] infrastructure modernization and expansion in these areas for the cities of the world will cost about $41 trillion—$15.8 trillion in Asia, $9.1 trillion in Europe, $7.4 trillion in Latin America, $6.5 trillion in the United States and Canada, $1.1 trillion in Africa, and $0.9 trillion in the Middle East. In the electricity sector, for example, the three geographical locales with the fastest-growing rate of electricity use are China, India, and Latin America. The International Energy Agency projects nearly

---

1   International Monetary Fund, *World Economic Outlook*, April 2008, 24.
2   Viren Doshi, Gary Schulman, and Daniel Gabaldon, "Lights! Water! Motion!" *Booz Allen Hamilton Strategy+Business*, No. 46 (Spring 2007): 3.

a tripling of electricity use in these markets between 2002 and 2030—from 4,500 terawatt-hours in 2002 to 12,000 in 2030.[3] A major determinant of the future developmental success and stability of these countries will be their ability to meet these infrastructure challenges.

TPCC Agency Initiatives

Many of the TPCC agencies have both trade and development mandates. A top priority of the Federal Government, therefore, is greater U.S. business involvement in major infrastructure and energy projects—both in the four priority markets covered in this chapter, and in the next generation markets highlighted in the next chapter. Crosscutting initiatives related to infrastructure and energy include:

WIREC: The 2008 Washington International Renewable Energy Conference (WIREC) was held in Washington, D.C., March 3–7, 2008. The event was co-sponsored by the United States Departments of Agriculture, Energy, and State, along with the American Council on Renewable Energy (ACORE). WIREC 2008 provided a global platform for government officials from the central to the local level to discuss with leaders from the private sector and civil society the integration of renewable energy everywhere. The conference included interactive sessions focused on creating the necessary enabling policy environment, financing, research and development, and deployment. In addition, a number of TPCC agencies organized a USA Pavillion at the trade show portion of the conference to highlight for the United States' renewable industry the types of assistance that are available for U.S. companies.

Global Conference on Agricultural Biofuels: USDA's Agricultural Research Service and FAS cosponsored, in cooperation with the University of Minnesota, a global biofuels conference on the science and technology of agriculturally-derived biofuels in Minneapolis, Minnesota, August 20–22, 2007. The objectives of the conference were to promote international scientific and technical cooperation in crafting common approaches and solutions to shared challenges in biofuels development. The conference also addressed the current and future state of biofuels research and development, the economics of biofuels production, and the environmental implications of biofuels. Leading scientists and policymakers from more than 40 countries attended the conference.

The Americas Competitiveness Forum—2008: The second annual Americas Competitiveness Forum (ACF) was held August 17–19, 2008, in Atlanta, Georgia (see www.CompetitivenessForum.com). The Forum provided an opportunity for governments, the business community, and representatives from academia and non-governmental organizations to discuss actions that can be taken to improve competitiveness and economic prosperity in the Americas. The 2008 ACF was held in partnership with the City of Atlanta and the International Training Center for Government Authorities (CIFAL Atlanta), a not-for-profit organization created by the United Nations. Atlanta Mayor Shirley Franklin is the Chair of CIFAL Atlanta's Board of Trustees, and co-hosted the ACF with Secretary of Commerce Carlos M. Gutierrez. More than 900 people from throughout the hemisphere participated in the 2008 ACF.

Clean Energy Trade Missions to China and India: In January 2008, U.S. Assistant Secretary of Commerce for Market Access and Compliance David Bohigian led 18 U.S. companies on the

---

3   Ibid., 6.

second U.S. Clean Energy Trade Mission. Mission stops included Beijing, Guangzhou, and Hong Kong, China; and Kolkata and Bangalore, India. The goal was to expose U.S. businesses to these fast-growing markets where American clean-energy technology goods and services can help improve the environment. Participating companies represented renewable energy, energy efficiency, clean coal, and distributed generation sectors. All companies participating in the mission belong to industry sectors advanced by the Asia Pacific Partnership on Clean Development and Climate (APP). The APP is a Presidential priority to achieve a reduction in the intensity of carbon dioxide and other greenhouse gas emissions and enhance energy security in the context of sustained economic growth. In September 2008, Assistant Secretary Bohigian led a third mission to China and India.

Nuclear Power in Emerging/Developing World: As part of the Bush Administration's plan for meeting energy needs around the world while reducing greenhouse gases, the United States has committed to work with nations that have advanced civilian nuclear energy programs. This partnership will work to provide the cheap and safe energy that growing economies need, while reducing the risk of nuclear proliferation and avoiding greenhouse gas emissions. A four-part strategy is being developed to address worldwide energy needs through the promotion of U.S. nuclear energy solutions. The elements are:

- creation of a TPCC interagency working group on civil nuclear trade to coordinate U.S. Government international policy and activities affecting U.S. civil nuclear trade;

- establishment of a U.S. civil nuclear industry advisory committee to advise the TPCC interagency group on U.S. foreign policy and programs that affect industry's competitiveness;

- promotion of U.S. industry at the International Atomic Energy Agency's fall General Conference; and

- announcement of a civil nuclear trade mission to a country of interest to industry.

President's Export Council (PEC) Recommendations: In 2008, the PEC continued its focus on Brazil, Russia, India, and China—the so-called "BRIC" countries—during its members' service to this Administration. The PEC has approved letters of recommendation regarding the U.S. trade and economic relationship with China (including a fact-finding trip in June 2004), Russia, and India, as well as bilateral investment treaties (BITs) with the BRIC nations.

CHINA

China's exceptional economic growth continues as the country further integrates with the global economy. U.S. companies are benefiting, as evidenced by rapid and sustained increases in U.S. exports to China (*Chart 12*). Over the past several years, the annual growth rate of U.S. exports to China averaged well over 20 percent. According to the Census Bureau, U.S. exports to China increased by 18.2 percent in 2007, helping to make China the fastest-growing foreign market for U.S. goods. The total China-U.S. trade is $386.7 billion, placing China as our second-biggest trading partner, behind Canada. Although U.S. imports of Chinese goods greatly exceed U.S. exports to China, China is our third-largest export market. U.S. merchandise exports to China reached a record $65.2 billion in 2007.

China's robust economy had a growth rate of 11.9 percent in 2007. The nation's rate of consumer consumption increased by an estimated 16.3 percent for the period of January through September 2007, according to a report by the Chinese Academy of Social Sciences (CASS). Despite remarkable change, China is still a developing country, with per capita income around $1,700. Yet surprisingly, the country stands as the world's third-largest market for luxury goods, behind Japan and the United States. Some studies estimate that more than 200 million Chinese citizens have a per capita income more than $8,000. China's per capita income figures are poised to change dramatically, as many economists predict a surge in the number of people achieving middle-class status.

China has been a priority market of the TPCC for the last four years. During that time, the TPCC put in place the most extensive trade promotion infrastructure in our global network. China is the largest post in the world for both the Foreign Agricultural Service (five offices and 49 staff) and the Department of Commerce (six offices and 140 staff). In addition, the Commercial Service offers its services through American Trading Centers in 14 secondary cities.

The TPCC agencies will focus their trade promotion resources on ensuring that U.S. companies are aware of the opportunities in China, understand and have the tools to address intellectual property rights issues, and are in position to take advantage of the continued need for improved infrastructure, more energy, better healthcare, and increased tourism.

CHART 12
U.S. MERCHANDISE EXPORTS TO CHINA, 1990-2007

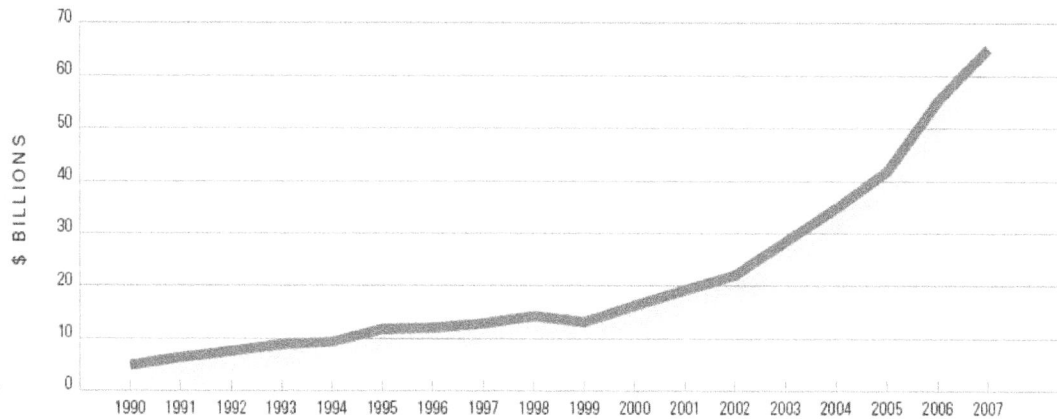

Source: U.S. Department of Commerce, Bureau of the Census.

TPCC Agency Initiatives

U.S.-China Ten-Year Energy and Environment Cooperation: In June 2008, Treasury Secretary Henry Paulson and Chinese Vice-Premier Wang Qishan signed a Ten-Year Energy and Environment Cooperation Framework that will foster trade in energy and environmental goods and services. By signing the Ten-Year Framework, which is an outcome of the U.S.-China Strategic Economic Dialogue, China has committed to engage in extensive collaboration to address the challenges of environmental sustainability, climate change, and energy security. Continued engagement with China under the Framework will open new export markets for U.S. businesses and expand private sector networks. The United States and China have launched joint research on alternative and renewable fuels for transportation, and are developing action plans on clean water, air, transportation, electricity, and conservation of forest and wetland ecosystems. The Framework also provides the United States with the opportunity to urge China to join a multilateral effort to eliminate restrictions on the trade of energy and environmental goods.

Second U.S.-China ACE Services Best Practices Exchange: In an effort to address barriers faced by U.S. architecture, construction, and engineering (ACE) companies in China, the Departments of State and Commerce and the Office of the U.S. Trade Representative engaged the Ministry of Construction (MOC) in the Second U.S.-China ACE Services Best Practices Exchange (BPE2) on March 4, 2008. Like the first exchange in 2007, BPE2 focused on ACE-sector best practices in project delivery and professional licensing to encourage the MOC to adopt measures that would facilitate export of U.S. ACE services. U.S. industry continues to show strong support for the BPE, which will hold its third meeting early next year in Beijing.

U.S.-China Biofuels Agreement: On the margins of the December 2007 meeting of the U.S.-China Joint Commission on Commerce and Trade (JCCT), three entities—USDA, the Department of Energy, and China's National Development and Reform Commission (NDRC)—signed a memorandum of understanding (MOU) that strengthens and expands cooperation on biofuels production and use. More specifically, the MOU encourages cooperation in biomass and feedstock production and sustainability, conversion technology and engineering, bio-based product development and utilization standards, and rural and agricultural development strategies. The MOU stands to benefit U.S. and Chinese agricultural producers. Increased cooperation, dialogue, exchanges, and projects facilitated by the MOU may result in new markets and uses for agricultural commodities and their waste products.

Health Care Mission: In April 2008, U.S. Under Secretary of Commerce for International Trade Christopher A. Padilla led 15 U.S. companies on a Health Care Mission to Beijing, China, in sectors including pharmaceuticals, medical devices, health insurance, and health services. China is considering significant changes to the financing, regulation, and management of its health care system. Participants had the opportunity to discuss these pending health care reforms with key officials from the Ministry of Health, Ministry of Finance, the State Food and Drug Administration, and others.

U.S.-China Tourism Agreement: In December 2007, Secretary of Commerce Carlos M. Gutierrez signed an MOU that will bring more customers to the U.S. tourism industry by facilitating both group leisure travel from China to the United States and U.S. industry and destination marketing efforts in China. The agreement between the United States and China was announced at the U.S.-China JCCT and was implemented in June 2008 in nine Chinese provinces. After a period of evaluation, the implementation will be extended to include all of China. The U.S. travel and tourism industry will benefit from this MOU. Chinese visits to the United States, forecasted to double by 2017, will significantly expand travel and tourism-related exports.

Power Plant Emissions Monitoring and Control Technologies Orientation Visit: In October 2008, a USTDA-funded orientation visit will host up to 11 officials from China's Ministry of Environmental Protection and from national and provincial environmental monitoring centers. These centers are responsible for enforcing established emissions regulations and are expected to be involved in substantial procurements of monitoring and control systems. Many of China's coal-fired power plants have not been outfitted with equipment to monitor and control harmful emissions, especially of nitrogen oxide and particulate matter. This visit to Washington, D.C.; Raleigh-Durham, North Carolina; and Pittsburgh, Pennsylvania will introduce the delegation to the U.S. Government agencies that regulate and promote emissions reductions, as well as to U.S. producers of equipment and services in this sector.

Intellectual Property Rights (IPR) Cooperation and Outreach: The United States continues to work with China on a range of intellectual property protection and enforcement matters, and supports robust engagement with China on IPR via bilateral dialogues, including the JCCT, and the Strategic Economic Dialogue (SED).

- At the December 2007 meeting of the JCCT, China agreed to work on a number of intellectual property (IP) issues with the United States, including exchanging information on customs seizures to focus China's enforcement resources further on companies exporting such goods; strengthening enforcement of laws against company name misuse; addressing loopholes in the regulation of bulk chemicals used in pharmaceuticals; and eliminating the requirement to submit viable biotech seeds for testing, which reduces the possibility of illegal copying of patented agricultural materials. The TPCC agencies are working to support follow-up activities related to these commitments.

- The Department of Commerce is leading the coordination of an IPR technical assistance conference to be held in Beijing in December 2008. The conference will bring together governments, including the United States, EU, and China's State Intellectual Property Office, as well as industry, academia, and multilateral institutions. Participants will identify ongoing IPR technical assistance efforts in China; areas in which more capacity building is needed; and mechanisms for enhancing coordination among providers and recipients of IPR technical assistance in China.

- The Department of Commerce, the American Bar Association, the National Association of Manufacturers, and the American Chamber of Commerce in China will continue to support the China IPR Advisory Program, which helps match SMEs with volunteer attorneys knowledgeable in China IPR issues for a free one-hour legal consultation. In 2007, more than 60 SMEs utilized the China IPR Advisory Program.

- The Department of Commerce will continue to present a monthly China IPR Webinar series for SMEs, having conducted 10 such Webinars in 2007.

"The Chinese are purchasing expensive new vehicles and people want to take care of their cars and make them last longer, so they want a quality product, and are willing to pay for it. However, we knew China was a potentially rewarding market with many challenges, and developing key relationships and trust with potential buyers was a priority."
—David Graham, Chairman and CEO

Lubri-Loy, Inc., is a Missouri manufacturer of automotive lubricants, including fuel additives and oil fortifiers. In 2003, Graham participated in a State of Missouri trade mission to China. The Commercial Service in St. Louis also encouraged Lubri-Loy to sign up for the Gold Key Program for pre-arranged business appointments with overseas distributors and agents. Lubri-Loy now has several distributors in China, including taxi stands and independent gas stations. Lubri-Loy also continues to build a strong brand name in Beijing, including the "automotive city" sector where there are hundreds of parts suppliers. China continues to be Lubri-Loy's fastest growing market, and the firm plans to expand beyond Beijing to China's second-tier markets such as Kunming, Dalian, Harbin, and other cities in the near future.

Agricultural Market Access Efforts: FAS provided critical input and support to several market access requests in 2007. Some of the issues resolved include China's agreeing: to allow six U.S. pork processing facilities to resume exports to China; to remove "contract value" requirements from draft agricultural licensing regulations that would have required U.S. farmers and agricultural exporters to disclose confidential business information; and, to eliminate the requirement to submit viable biotech seeds for testing. Many of these issues were previously raised in various bilateral technical fora, but for the most part required political-level intervention in order to reach an agreement.

Sanitary/Phytosanitary (SPS) Technical Cooperation: The United States and China are engaged in a series of technical exchanges aimed at helping Chinese officials gain a better understanding of the principles and application of the WTO/SPS Agreement, and to apply these SPS principles to support science-based systems. These exchanges included a WTO/SPS Leadership Development Program with China, a Joint Institute for Food Safety and Applied Nutrition Risk Assessment Training Course, and other collaboration in the area of food safety. USDA also offers a variety of programs to promote scientific and technical cooperation with China, such as the Scientific Cooperation Research Program. This cooperation supports U.S. agricultural priorities, encourages long-term cooperation in agricultural science and technology, creates a positive atmosphere for agricultural trade, and enhances overall bilateral relations.

Trade Shows: The Commercial Service staff in China will be working to identify and promote areas of opportunities for U.S. companies. A principal means for accomplishing this objective will be to encourage U.S. companies to participate in the U.S. pavilion at one of the major trade shows in China. Trade shows the Commercial Service will promote include: The Sino-Dental Meeting, China International Equipment Manufacturing Exposition, The China Power, Oil & Gas Expo 2008, and the China International Food Quality & Safety Expo.

INDIA

The Indian market, and its one-billion-plus population, presents lucrative and diverse opportunities for U.S. exporters. Since 2005, the Indian economy has grown by more than 9 percent a year, and in spite of the global slowdown, is expected to continue growing by about 8 percent through 2009 and beyond.[4] In 2007, U.S. exports to India reached a record $17.6 billion—a 75 percent increase over $10.1 billion in 2006 (*Chart 13*). With U.S. exports growing at a much steeper rate than imports, the bilateral trade deficit with India fell by almost half, from $11.8 billion in 2006 to $6.5 billion in 2007.

As the commercial engagement of India and the United States grows, the two countries continue to strengthen their economic ties through several bilateral dialogues, including the Commercial Dialogue, the Trade Policy Forum, the CEO Forum, and the U.S.-India High-Technology Cooperation Group, to name a few. These dialogues are helping to improve the transparency and predictability of the commercial environment. The Commercial Dialogue has been extended through March 2010 and covers intellectual property rights, standards, technical exchanges on antidumping/countervailing duty practices, and small and medium-sized enterprises. In addition, we will be seeking ways to use collaborative mechanisms, such as our Total Economic Engagement projects, to help improve the climate for U.S. business and foster more partnerships between the U.S. and Indian private sectors.

In addition to the focus on improving the commercial relationship, our priority will be to focus on India's infrastructure needs. Various estimates show that India will need to spend $300 to $900 billion on infrastructure improvements over the next six years. The Department of the Treasury, the Department of Commerce, Ex-Im Bank, USTDA, the Department of Agriculture, the Department of Transportation, and the Department of Energy are all playing a role in this endeavor. Much of this effort started in October 2007 when U.S. Treasury Secretary Henry Paulson and Ex-Im Bank Chairman James Lambright participated in the U.S.-India CEO Forum Infrastructure Investment Conference in Mumbai.

4 International Monetary Fund, *World Economic Outlook*, April 2008.

CHART 13
U.S. MERCHANDISE EXPORTS TO INDIA, 1990-2007

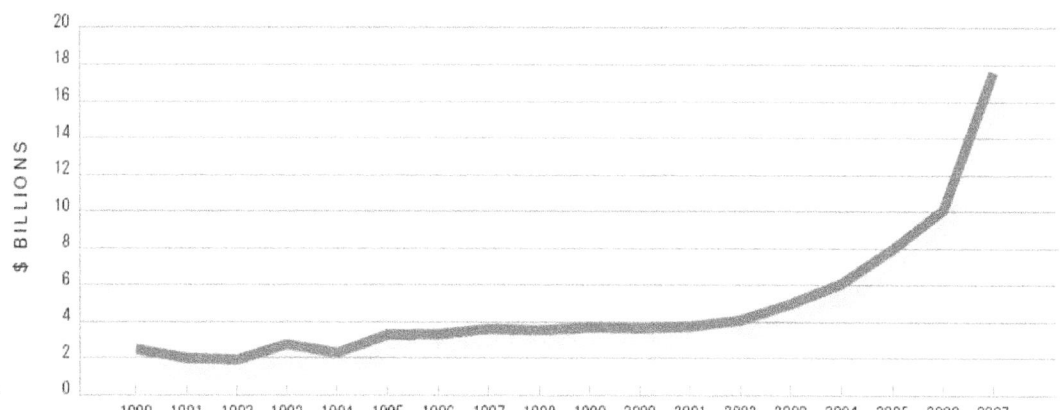

Source: U.S. Department of Commerce, Bureau of the Census.

TPCC Agency Activities

Ex-Im Bank Facility for Indian Infrastructure Initiative: In April 2008, Ex-Im Bank approved a $2.2 billion Indian Infrastructure Facility that will support U.S. exports to Indian projects in sectors such as power and renewable energy generation, oil and gas development, small aircraft, airport development, and health care. Under the facility, eight Indian financial institutions provide their guarantees to expedite processing of Ex-Im Bank-backed medium-term and long-term financing for Indian buyers of U.S. exports.

In addition, Ex-Im Bank has been working to establish partnerships with business, government, and financial institutions in India. In March 2008, Ex-Im Bank Board Member Diane Farrell and staff conducted business development meetings, focusing on SMEs, with officials in Hyderabad, Pune, Mumbai, and New Delhi. The first transaction under the new facility supported a $29.4 million long-term loan guarantee to support multiple exports of U.S. medical, building, and office equipment and services for the construction of Bhopal Medical College in Bhopal, India.

U.S.-India Energy Dialogue: USTDA and the Department of Energy are supporting the U.S.-India Energy Dialogue. The Dialogue promotes increased trade and investment in the energy sector by working with the public and private sectors to further identify areas of collaboration. This year, USTDA has approved seven activities for funding.

- A $628,926 grant in April 2008 to the Hindustan Petroleum Corporation Limited (HPCL) for technical assistance. The grant will be used to introduce the company to a wide range of advanced safety technologies and inspection methodologies.

- A $348,339 grant to India's Petroleum and Natural Gas Regulatory Board. The grant partially funds technical assistance for midstream and downstream oil and gas regulation capacity building. The contractor, the National Association of Regulatory Utility Commissioners, is contributing an additional $141,600 in the form of expert labor services.

- A $597,892 grant to HPCL for a detailed evaluation of technologies for converting low-value residual oil products (refinery bottoms) to higher value products for the Indian market. The grant partially funds a study awarded by HPCL to Kellogg, Brown, and Root (KBR) to perform the study. Both HPCL and KBR will be contributing additional resources to the activity.

- A $370,000 grant to Bharat Petroleum Corporation Limited (BPCL) to partially fund technical assistance for an asset integrity management project for its petroleum refineries and associated pipelines. Assistance includes training on advanced methods for conducting comprehensive inspection programs. BPCL is contributing an additional $63,310.

- A $180,578 transfer to the Minerals Management Service (MMS) of thc U.S. Department of the Interior to fund technical assistance for India's Oil Industry Safety Directorate. MMS will carry out joint offshore safety audits and inspections, training programs, and workshops.

- A $600,000 grant to Reliance Industries Limited to partially fund a feasibility study for a lignite/petroleum residue-to-synthetic liquid fuel project. The study will consider the application of advanced proprietary coal-to-liquids technology from Headwaters CTL, LLC, a U.S. firm based in Utah, with laboratories in New Jersey. Reliance is contributing an additional $391,305 and Headwaters an additional $120,000.

- A $256,142 grant to Binani Cement Limited for a feasibility study to evaluate alternate mining technology for a captive mining concession supporting its cement plant. This project is expected to serve as a template for other Indian companies. Gustavson Associates, of Boulder, Colorado, is performing the study.

Commercial Service Infrastructure Trade Promotion and Project Development Initiative: The Commercial Service is utilizing its seven offices in India to tap infrastructure opportunities across the country. Special project teams focused on airports, rail, mass transit, energy, and the environment identify the most promising opportunities for U.S. companies, qualify local partners who can represent U.S. firms or participate in joint ventures, and disseminate information about the projects to U.S. financial companies, developers, equipment suppliers, and design and engineering firms. Valuable early alerts and project developments are "pushed" to U.S. firms through consultations directly with U.S. firms as well as through Webinars, conferences in the United States, trade leads, and reverse trade missions to the United States. The Commercial Service will be teaming with national and local partners to better position U.S. companies in the following ways:

- Partner with a major U.S. consulting firm to survey the market. Meetings are held with project owners; project briefs are developed; and market information is disseminated to U.S. firms through ITA industry teams.

- Support Government of India infrastructure development efforts by agreeing to government agency requests for the United States to become the "partner-country" for key infrastructure conferences and exhibitions that are government priorities. In addition to creating USA Pavilions at these events, the Commercial Service is working with U.S. industry associations to bring trade missions to these exhibitions and conferences. This facilitates greater access for U.S. firms to central and state government decision makers, increases dialogue opportunities at conferences, roundtables and networking events, and enhances U.S.-India collaborative efforts on best practices, technology, and systems.

- Encourage U.S. States and regional and local development agencies to organize trade missions to India and include strong infrastructure-related activities in these programs. Missions can include representatives from airports, seaports, rail, financial services, and economic development agencies that can share best practices and profile U.S. technology and expertise to solve major infrastructure problems.

- Collaborate closely with Ex-Im Bank and USTDA to identify infrastructure opportunities that offer potential for U.S. financing and technical assistance.

U.S.-India Aviation Cooperation Program (ACP): The ACP—a public-private partnership between USTDA, the U.S. Federal Aviation Administration (FAA), U.S. aviation companies, and the Indian aviation sector—provides a forum for unified communication between the Government of India and U.S. public and private sector entities. The ACP is designed to work directly with the Indian government to identify and support India's civil aviation sector modernization priorities. The India Air Traffic Management Training Program (ATMTP) is the first activity under the ACP. An orientation visit to the United States in May 2008 focused on improving high-density air traffic management operations at leading Indian airports as India's aviation sector continues to manage rapid growth and modernization. The program

EXPORT SUCCESS

LINCOLN ELECTRIC, Cleveland, Ohio

"By increasing exports of our high technology products, we not only add to our top line, but also maintain and increase the number of manufacturing jobs here in the United States. Our employees continue to demonstrate America's competitiveness on the global markets."
—John Stopki, Chairman and CEO

Lincoln Electric is a worldwide leader in production of welding equipment, with subsidiary companies around the globe. Bharat Heavy Electrical Ltd (BHEL), an Indian firm, contacted the Commercial Service in India for help in sourcing U.S. products and services related to energy generation, development, renovation and maintenance. Commercial Service India arranged for representatives from BHEL to visit potential suppliers in the United States. As a result of their visit, Lincoln Electric made a sale and established a relationship with BHEL. In May 2007, Commerce Secretary Carlos M. Gutierrez joined President Bush at the White House to present Lincoln Electric with the Presidential "E" Award for excellence in exporting, one of the highest honors the Federal Government can give to an American exporting company.

included visits by senior officials of the Airports Authority of India and the Directorate General of Civil Aviation to four U.S. cities—Washington, D.C.; Atlantic City, New Jersey; Orlando, Florida; and Atlanta, Georgia—to demonstrate procedures, regulations, and private-public cooperation for high density operations. The ATMTP program also included a two-week Operational Workshop in August 2008 for air traffic controllers.

India Cold Chain Training Program and Orientation Visit: In October-November 2008, USTDA is sponsoring a program to strengthen India's cold chain infrastructure by providing state-of-the-art training to stakeholders in the Indian cold chain sector regarding proper post-harvest handling, transportation, and storage of fresh fruits and vegetables and other perishable commodities. USTDA held a series of cold chain workshops in India (Chennai and Mumbai in November-December 2007, and New Delhi and Kolkata in March 2008), and will sponsor a U.S. study tour in October-November 2008 for a select group of workshop attendees to receive more specialized training.

Agricultural Knowledge Initiative: Launched in July 2005, the U.S.-India Agricultural Knowledge Initiative (AKI) is led by USDA. AKI facilitates technology transfer, trade, and investment, and bolsters agricultural research, education, and extension through public-private partnerships.

U.S.-India Trade Policy Forum (TPF): Launched in July 2005 and led by the Office of the U.S. Trade Representative (USTR), the TPF serves as the umbrella forum overseeing the U.S.-India trade agenda with the objective of enhancing the pace of growth in our bilateral trade. The TPF has five focus groups: Agriculture; Innovation and Creativity (intellectual property rights); Investment; Services; and Tariff and Non-Tariff Barriers. The focus groups meet on a regular basis—in person and by digital video conference—to discuss a range of trade policy issues that impact trade and investment flows between the United States and India. Notable successes include facilitating U.S. almond and apple exports to India, adoption of appropriate emission standards on motorcycles, and the exploratory talks on a Bilateral Investment Treaty (BIT). In addition, a Private Sector Advisory Group of U.S. and Indian private sector trade experts was created in 2007 to provide strategic analysis and recommendations to the TPF on potential building blocks for the bilateral economic and trade relationship.

The Validated End-User (VEU) Program: In October 2007, the Department of Commerce's Bureau of Industry and Security (BIS) announced that Indian companies were eligible to participate in the VEU program, an innovative export control mechanism that will facilitate high-technology exports from the United States to India. Under the program, BIS authorizes participating companies to receive shipments of specified items under a general authorization instead of under multiple individual export licenses, thus relieving the companies of the administrative and regulatory burden associated with individual export licenses. Companies interested in participating in the VEU program must submit a detailed application to BIS; the application is reviewed by an interagency committee, and successful applicants are notified through publication in the *Federal Register*. BIS is currently reviewing the first groups of applicants for participation in the program and anticipates publication of their names in fall 2008.

Commercial Service India Business Center: In June 2008, the Commercial Service launched the new India Business Center (IBC), housed in the Trade Information Center. The IBC joins the two existing business information centers—the China Business Information Center (China BIC) and the Middle East and North Africa Business Information Center (MENA BIC)—in providing specialized assistance to U.S. exporters. The IBC's mission is to help U.S. companies take advantage of the growing market opportunities for export to India and provide market intelligence and other information critical to the success of American companies in India. The IBC is also dedicated to helping U.S. companies overcome challenges to accessing the Indian market, including tariff and non-tariff barriers to trade, complex regulations, and infrastructure weaknesses. The IBC maintains a Web portal grouping all the information available about doing business in India, provides specialized telephone counseling on the market via 1-800-USA-TRAD(E), and performs outreach activities to raise U.S. business awareness of opportunities in India.

BRAZIL

In 2007, economic growth in Brazil accelerated appreciably—from 3.8 percent in 2006 to 5.4 percent in 2007—supported in part by declining interest rates, strong employment, and the resulting strong domestic demand.[5] With a GDP of $1.3 trillion,[6] Brazil represents roughly half of the South American territory and economy. The country is rich in agricultural, mineral, and industrial resources, and offers substantial market opportunities for U.S. exporters in a diverse array of sectors that support Brazil's drive to industrialize further, attract energy and transportation investment, and promote its exports. The United States continues to be Brazil's single largest trading partner. Record U.S. exports of $24.6 billion in 2007 represented a 28 percent increase over 2006 (*Chart 14*). Moreover, the bilateral trade deficit with Brazil shrank dramatically in 2007 to $1 billion from $7.1 billion in 2006.

---

5 International Monetary Fund, *World Economic Outlook*, April 2008, 82.

6 International Monetary Fund, *World Economic Outlook* Database, April 2008 (2007, current prices).

While there are significant opportunities for U.S. companies in Brazil, these firms often face challenges. Taxes on imports are high, and there are also significant government regulations and confusing product standards. In addition to focusing policy discussions with the Brazilians on these issues, the TPCC agencies are focusing their activities on getting more U.S. companies to participate in Brazilian infrastructure development.

TPCC Agency Activities

U.S.-Brazil Infrastructure Initiative: In March 2007 Brazilian President Luiz Inácio Lula da Silva expressed interest to President George W. Bush in tapping into U.S. expertise to help Brazil pursue regional integration and development of its infrastructure. In particular, Brazil needs to improve its transportation and energy infrastructure. In response, the Treasury Department has put together an interagency working group that is looking at ways to increase U.S. companies' participation in priority Brazilian infrastructure projects.

U.S.-Brazil Commercial Dialogue: In June 2006, the U.S. Department of Commerce and the Brazilian Ministry for Industry, Development, and Commerce launched the U.S.-Brazil Commercial Dialogue to facilitate trading relations between the two countries. Key activities under the umbrella of this dialogue include customs facilitation, IPR protection, and export promotion. Results to date include collaboration between the United States Patent and Trademark Office and Brazil's National Institute of Industrial Property, which has resulted in several joint activities regarding patent and trademark issues. The Commerce and Customs authorities in both countries are working together in areas such as technical exchanges and orientation visits to express-delivery services facilities in support of Brazil's customs modernization goals. Other areas of collaboration include strengthening the partnership in franchising and identifying best practices to promote entrepreneurship, investment, and business skills.

Secretary Gutierrez Hosts U.S.-Brazil CEO Forum: In April 2008, Secretary of Commerce Carlos M. Gutierrez and Daniel Price, U.S. Assistant to the President for International Economic Affairs, hosted the second meeting of the U.S.-Brazil CEO Forum in Washington, D.C. At the Forum, the U.S. and Brazilian governments reported to the 10 U.S. and 10

CHART 14

U.S. MERCHANDISE EXPORTS TO BRAZIL, 1990–2007

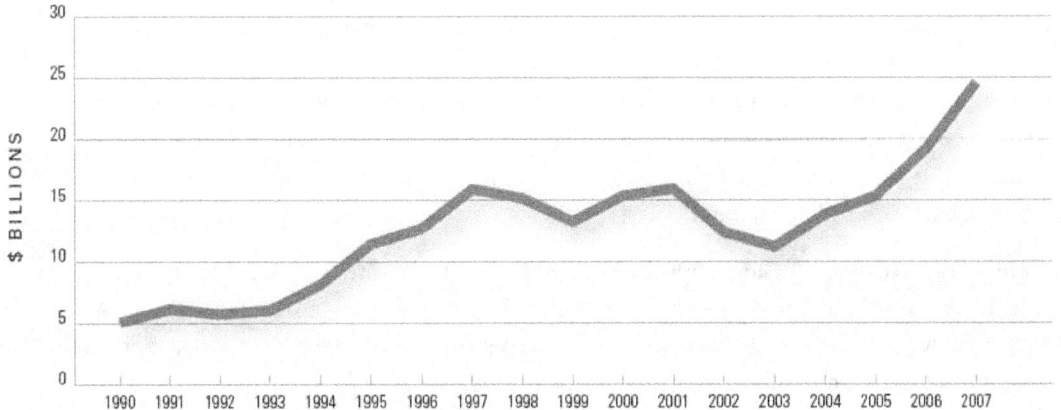

Source: U.S. Department of Commerce, Bureau of the Census.

*Press Conference on October 11, 2007, at the inaugural meeting of the U.S.-Brazil CEO Forum in Brasilia. From left to right: **Josué Christiano Gomes da Silva**, Chairman and CEO, Coteminas S.A. (Chair of the Brazilian Section); **Allan Hubbard**, then-U.S. National Economic Council Director; **Dilma Rousseff**, Brazil's Casa Civil Minister; **Carlos M. Gutierrez**, U.S. Secretary of Commerce; **Miguel Jorge**, Brazil's Minister of Development, Industry and Foreign Trade; and **Tim Solso**, Chairman and CEO, Cummins Inc. (Chair of the U.S. Section).*

Brazilian CEOs on progress made on the CEOs' priority issues, including a bilateral tax treaty, a bilateral investment treaty, visas, infrastructure, and the Doha Round.

USTDA Promotion of Intelligent Transportation System in Brazil: In September 2007 USTDA awarded a grant to Belo Horizonte Traffic and Transportation Company in Brazil to facilitate traffic management through the expansion of intelligent transportation systems. The $294,000 grant will fund an evaluation of a proposed expansion of an Intelligent Transportation System and Integrated Traffic Information Management System in Belo Horizonte, the fourth largest metropolitan area in Brazil.

Brazil Marginal Oil Fields Regulatory Orientation Visit: In June 2008, USTDA sponsored an orientation visit to the United States for Brazil's National Petroleum and Natural Gas Regulatory Agency to evaluate the U.S. regulatory framework governing marginal oil fields and to become familiar with U.S. companies active in this industry. The visit supports Brazil's efforts to promote exploration and production opportunities of on-shore marginal/ mature fields for SMEs. The delegation met with regulators and industry representatives in Washington, D.C.; Oklahoma; and Texas.

Natural Gas Regulatory Policies Orientation Visit: In November 2007, USTDA sponsored an orientation visit to the United States to familiarize Brazilian regulators with the U.S. regulatory framework governing natural gas. The visit focused particularly on the construction and operation of liquefied natural gas terminals, the operational security of oil and gas pipelines and terminals, and regulations for natural gas storage. The delegation met with U.S. public- and private-sector stakeholders in Washington, D.C., and Houston, Texas.

RUSSIA

In 2007, the Russian economy continued its sustained steady growth, with GDP growing by an estimated 8.1 percent. With GDP of about $1.3 trillion[7], Russia now ranks as one of the top ten economies in the world. While much of this growth is due to rising world prices for oil and natural gas, 2007 also saw the continued steady rise of consumer spending and a continued construction boom. Growth has spread well beyond Moscow and St. Petersburg to other regions and cities of one million inhabitants or more. Per capita GDP is estimated to have reached $9,050 in 2007 compared to $7,170 in 2006, leaving Russian consumers with disposable income for imported products.

According to the U.S. business community in Russia, the business environment is positive. In 2007, the American Chamber of Commerce surveyed U.S. companies currently operating in Russia and found that 50 percent report sales increases of 200 percent from 2001 to 2005; profitability during 2001-2005 was on or above target; and 67 percent expect sales growth of more than 50 percent through 2008. In 2007 U.S. merchandise exports to Russia reached a record $7.4 billion—a 57 percent increase over 2006 (*Chart 15*).

There are strong growth possibilities in a range of consumer goods and services, which are being fueled by increases in disposable income in Moscow, St. Petersburg, and the grow- ing regional centers. This includes telecommunications equipment and services, especially wireless, autos and parts, computer hardware and software, cosmetics and toiletries, and building products. Thanks to continuing budget surpluses, the Russian Government has created a number of industrial development funds which will be used to facilitate the mod- ernization of Russia's industrial base. These investments are creating growing opportunities for the U.S. machine tool and manufacturing service sectors. In addition, we expect to see strong growth in the energy, machinery, and healthcare sectors.

7 International Monetary Fund, *World Economic Outlook Database*, April 2008 (2007, current prices).

CHART 15
U.S. MERCHANDISE EXPORTS TO RUSSIA, 1992-2007

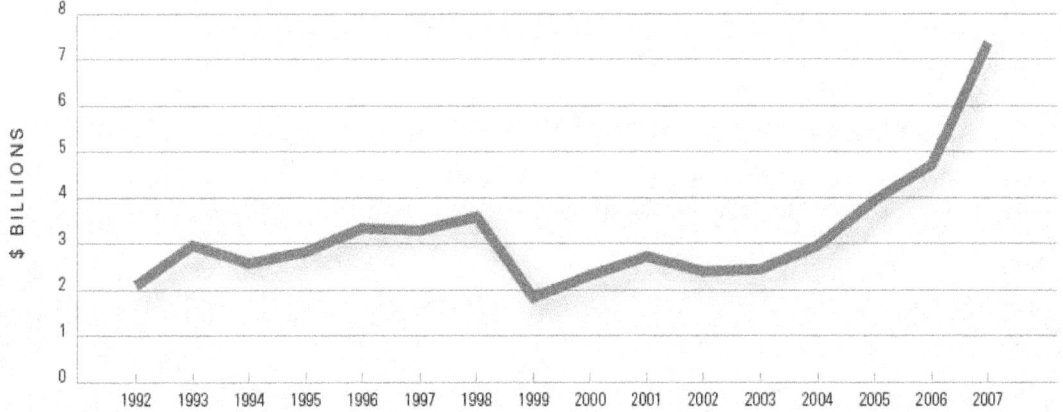

Source: U.S. Department of Commerce, Bureau of the Census.

The major barriers to the Russian market are: increased business costs for doing business in major cities; a weak judicial system; corruption, particularly when product certification or licensing is involved; and issues arising from customs clearance. However, the new Strategic Sectors Law, outlining procedures and restrictions on foreign investment in key sectors such as the extractive, defense, and telecommunications industries, is viewed by the foreign investment community as offering greater transparency while reducing bureaucratic procedures. The U.S. Government has been addressing barriers U.S. companies face in key sectors through direct U.S.-Russia interaction, but rising tensions between Russia and the international community threaten to undermine progress that has been made and increases uncertainty for those doing business in the country.

TPCC Agency Activities

U.S.-Russia Economic Dialogue: The inaugural U.S.-Russia Economic Dialogue was held on April 28, 2008, in Washington, D.C. The dialogue was co-chaired by Under Secretary for Economic, Energy and Agricultural Affairs Reuben Jeffery III and Deputy Foreign Minister Andrey Denisov. The dialogue was the first tangible outcome of the Strategic Framework Agreement, signed by Presidents Putin and Bush in Sochi in early April 2008, and the first of three dialogues to be launched as a part of the Framework (the others are private sector business and energy dialogues). The agenda for the day included a presentation on the U.S. economy, a discussion of open investment policy, and a discussion of sovereign wealth funds. Participants also discussed energy efficiency and exchanged views on the structure of the business-to-business dialogue.

PEC Mission to Russia: Several PEC members accompanied Secretary of Commerce Carlos M. Gutierrez to Kyiv, Ukraine, and St. Petersburg, Russia, June 4–7, 2008. The PEC members participated in the Twelfth Annual St. Petersburg International Economic Forum and met with government and private sector representatives in both locations to assess the opportunities, as well as the challenges, in both markets. The PEC members also received briefings from U.S. diplomats and business executives to gain further insight into both markets. Upon their return, the PEC members drafted and approved a letter of recommendation to the President with suggestions on ways to improve our trade and economic relationships with the two countries.

Agricultural Market Access: FAS monitored the implementation of the agricultural elements under the U.S.-Russia Bilateral Market Access Agreement, signed in November 2006. Tangible market access benefits included the reopening of the Russian market to U.S. beef, including the listing of 18 U.S. processing establishments for participation in trade; the significant expansion of U.S. pork into the Russian retail market through the removal of trichinae restrictions and USDA's authority to list U.S. establishments for participation in trade; a record high for U.S. poultry exports to Russia related to USDA's authority to list U.S. establishments for participation in trade; and the establishment of a Consultative Mechanism to discuss issues related to trade in biotech products.

Next Generation Markets

Although a few large countries like China and India have led the pace, most emerging and developing countries have maintained strong growth in recent years. As a group, the emerging and developing countries did even better in 2007 than in 2006, with 7.9 percent growth.[1] Financial turbulence in the advanced countries has prompted the lowering of forecasts. Yet emerging and developing countries are experiencing fewer spillover effects than in previous episodes.[2] As a result, these markets are expected to continue achieving impressive growth rates exceeding 6.5 percent in both 2008 and 2009.[3]

Two main factors underpin this growth. First, developing countries are increasingly integrated into the global economy, bolstered by stronger macroeconomic frameworks and business environments. Second, many countries—including those in Africa, Latin America, and the Middle East—are benefiting from broad-based commodity price increases which have fueled their exports and investment. Along with increases in intra-regional trade and diversification into manufacturing exports, these countries have become less dependent on the business cycle of the advanced countries.[4] With much of Latin America already the focus of the National Export Strategy in the Free Trade Agreements and Priority Markets chapters, this chapter focuses on Africa and the Middle East, both of which are expected to have growth topping 6 percent in 2008.

GLOBAL PARTNERSHIP ENSURES AVAILABILITY OF EXPORT ASSISTANCE

In April 2008, the Commercial Service and the U.S. Department of State agreed to provide Commercial Service-branded products and services to the U.S. business community at more than 100 embassies that do not have a Department of Commerce presence. This formal relationship will greatly improve the 85 existing Joint Commercial Service-State Post Partnership programs worldwide. These programs are designed to establish regional working arrangements whereby embassies without a Commercial Service presence can better assist

---

1 Country classification in the International Monetary Fund's *World Economic Outlook* divides the world into two major groups: advanced economies and emerging and developing economies. Rather than being based on strict criteria, economic or otherwise, this classification has evolved over time. Under these classifications, there are currently 31 advanced economies and 141 emerging and developing economies. (See International Monetary Fund, *World Economic Outlook*, Statistical Appendix, April 2008, 229-239).

2 Ibid. 22.

3 Ibid. xv.

4 Ibid. 24.

the U.S. business community. State Department economic Foreign Service Officers at these embassies will draw on the expertise and information technology systems of nearby embassies that have a Commercial Service presence, as well as on Commercial Service offices in Washington, D.C. With this renewed focus on establishing a global delivery of branded Commercial Service products and services, a baseline level of support will be available for U.S. companies regardless of country.

THE MIDDLE EAST AND NORTH AFRICA

The Middle East and North Africa have maintained a strong and healthy pace of economic growth. In oil-exporting countries, governments are spending more on infrastructure and social projects, and expanded credit in the private sector is driving domestic spending and imports. Outside of the oil-producing states, economic growth can be even stronger, driven in part by domestic reforms and spillover effects from the oil-producing states that are investing in the region. Egypt's economy, for example, grew by more than 7 percent in 2007.[5] As a result, the Middle Eastern countries, including Egypt, registered economic growth of 5.8 percent in both 2006 and 2007, with growth forecast to accelerate to 6.1 percent in both 2008 and 2009.[6]

In 2007, U.S. exports to the Middle East and North Africa grew 22 percent to $55.6 billion (*Chart 16*).

- In the Middle Eastern countries, sectors with the biggest share of overall U.S. exports were machinery (20 percent), aircraft and aircraft parts (15 percent), and vehicles (14 percent). Of top exporting sectors by value, those with the highest rates of growth from 2006 to 2007 include miscellaneous chemicals (66 percent), cereals (63 percent), and machinery (52 percent).

- In North Africa, sectors with the biggest share of overall U.S. exports were cereals (26 percent) and machinery (18 percent). Of top exporting sectors by value, those with the

5 International Monetary Fund, *World Economic Outlook*, April 2008, 97.
6 Ibid., 98.

CHART 16
U.S. MERCHANDISE EXPORTS TO THE MIDDLE EAST AND NORTH AFRICA, 1990–2007

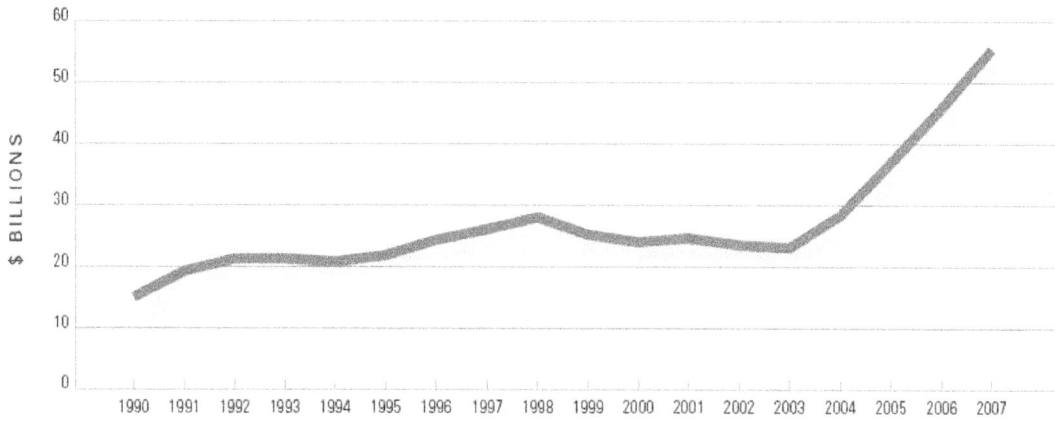

Source: U.S. Department of Commerce, Bureau of the Census.

highest rates of growth from 2006 to 2007 include mineral fuels (151 percent), cereals (104 percent), and plastics (85 percent).

Based on commercial developments in the Middle East and North Africa, the TPCC agencies are focusing their resources and coordination efforts on raising awareness of opportunities in the region among U.S. companies, and highlighting advantages that exist for U.S. companies in countries with which the United States has FTAs in place. These priorities are reflected in several recently implemented and planned initiatives of the TPCC agencies.

TPCC Agency Initiatives

U.S.-Middle East and North Africa Trade and Investment Conference: The U.S. Department of Commerce and the Business Council for International Understanding, in collaboration with the U.S.-Jordan Business Alliance, jointly organized a two-day conference at the Dead Sea in Jordan from February 10–11, 2008. The conference included keynote presentations by Secretary of Commerce Carlos M. Gutierrez, Jordanian Prime Minister Nader al-Dahabi, and Jordanian Minister of Industry and Trade Amer Hadidi; and was supported by the Aqaba Development Corporation, the Jordan Investment Bureau, and Enterprise Florida. Underwritten by 13 corporations, this unique gathering drew more than 250 business and political leaders from the United States, the Middle East, and North Africa. Participants exchanged ideas on expanding economic growth, commercial development within the region, and trade ties between the United States and countries of the Middle East and North Africa. Presentations and discussions focused on investment incentives; trade policy reforms; technology commercialization and transfer; and industry sectors critical to enhancing economic growth and development. Special sessions included information and communications technologies, health care, energy and water, transportation, logistics, and infrastructure. Participants identified significant business development leads and potential strategic partners, expanded their contacts, and accessed government decision-makers.

Secretary of Commerce Carlos M. Gutierrez addressing the U.S.-Middle East and North Africa Trade and Investment Conference, Dead Sea, Jordan, on February 11, 2008. Seated to his right: Mr. Don Pressley (Vice President, Booz Allen Hamilton); H.E. Amer Hadidi (Jordanian Minister of Industry and Trade); H.E. Eliyahu Yishai (Israeli Minister of Industry, Trade and Labor); H.E. Samir Abdallah (Palestinian Authority Minister of Planning); and H.E. Bouselham Hilia (Moroccan Secretary General, Ministry of Industry, Trade and New Technologies).

OPIC Access to Opportunity in the Middle East Conference: In May 2008, OPIC organized the "Access to Opportunity in the Middle East" international investment conference in Jordan. The conference highlighted investment opportunities in the region; encouraged the formation of joint ventures and partnerships between U.S. and local businesses; and facilitated support for new investments. The program itself included leading investment experts; U.S. businesses currently investing in the Middle East; financial institutions operating in the region; and U.S. Government officials. Sessions focused on access to credit, low- and middle-income housing, and infrastructure. Spotlighted sectors included tourism, information technology, franchising, and energy. Featured markets were Afghanistan, Bahrain, Egypt, Iraq, Israel, Jordan, Kuwait, Lebanon, Oman, West Bank and Gaza, and Yemen.

Business Development Mission to Saudi Arabia: In December 2007, the United States-Saudi Arabian Business Council, in collaboration with the U.S. Department of Commerce, organized a business development mission to Saudi Arabia. The mission was organized to provide U.S. companies with an opportunity to learn first-hand the substantial opportunities that exist within the booming Saudi market. Twenty-one executives representing nine U.S. companies participated in the mission. The Commercial Service in Saudi Arabia arranged more than 100 business meetings for mission members with local companies.

***Commercial News USA* Produces Arabic-Language Edition:** In response to growing demand for U.S.-made products and services in the Middle East, *Commercial News USA*, the official export promotion magazine of the Department of Commerce, has published its first-ever Arabic-language edition. Distributing a print magazine remains important in many markets, given that only 20 percent of the world's population currently has Internet access. Access is even lower in some rapidly developing regions, including the Middle East (2.5 percent) and Africa (3.4 percent).[7]

The Arabic version of *Commercial News USA* helps U.S. companies reach foreign businesses in their native language. More than 100 U.S. companies are included in the inaugural Arabic edition, which is available in print and online. The print version will reach readers in 16 Arabic-speaking countries, and the online version will be accessible to Arabic speakers worldwide. Targeted markets include the United Arab Emirates, Saudi Arabia, Kuwait, Egypt, and Jordan. *Commercial News USA* also has published Chinese- and Spanish-language editions. The English-language version, which is sent to 105,000 recipients, is published bimonthly. Electronic versions are available online at www.export.gov/cnusa.

SUB-SAHARAN AFRICA

Sub-Saharan Africa has been enjoying its best period of sustained economic growth in years, with 6.8 percent growth in 2007, thanks to the strong exports of commodity-producing countries; to strong domestic demand; and to foreign and domestic investment in non-commodity-producing countries.[8] Solid global demand for commodities, greater flows of capital to Africa, and debt relief have helped generate growth. Strengthened macroeconomic policies and years of structural reforms have begun to bear fruit. Not only have investment and growth increased, but income volatility has fallen to near 30-year lows. Not surprisingly, real

7 www.internetworldstats.com.

8 International Monetary Fund, *World Economic Outlook*, April 2008, 94-95.

CHART 17

U.S. MERCHANDISE EXPORTS TO SUB-SAHARAN AFRICA, 1990–2007

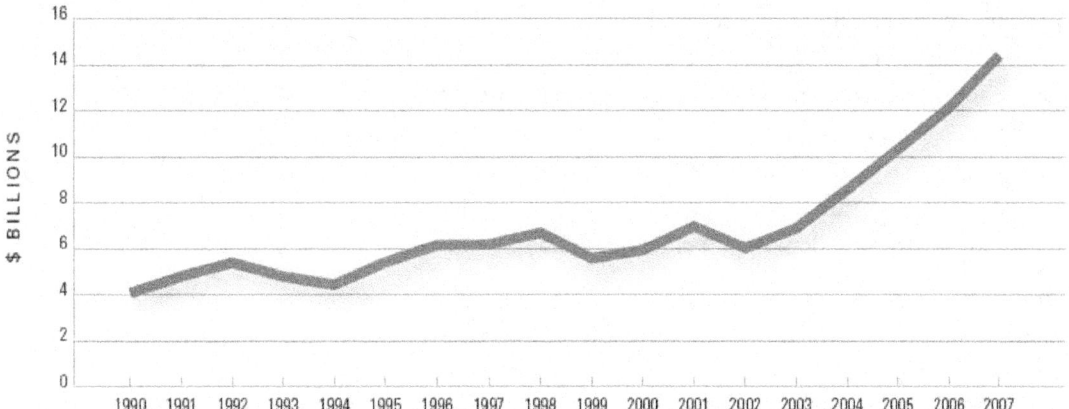

Source: U.S. Department of Commerce, Bureau of the Census.

per capita income is improving, although fragile countries continue to lag behind. Economic growth in sub-Saharan Africa is expected to remain at or above 6.6 percent in 2008 and 2009.[9]

In 2007, U.S. exports to sub-Saharan Africa increased 19 percent to $14.4 billion (*Chart 17*). The sectors with the biggest share of overall U.S. exports include machinery (24 percent), vehicles (15 percent), and cereals (8 percent). Of top exporting sectors by value, those with the highest rates of growth from 2006 to 2007 include ships and boats (681 percent), milling products (105 percent), and animal or vegetable fats (72 percent).

While per capita incomes are low throughout sub-Saharan Africa, these are countries where U.S. Government programs and services are important to ensuring that U.S. companies are able to navigate the markets and mitigate risk.

TPCC Agency Initiatives

Commerce Department/State Department Branding Africa Program: The "Branding Africa" program was recently launched in order to help U.S. companies take advantage of U.S. Government programs and assistance for exporting to Africa. The new Web site (www.export.gov/africa) links U.S. firms to embassies throughout Africa and to specific trade-related U.S. Government agencies, including the Commercial Service; FAS; OPIC; USTR; Ex-Im Bank; MCC; and the U.S. Agency for International Development (USAID) and its Trade Hubs, as well as other U.S. Government and non-government resources. The site directs U.S. firms to export assistance on sales, marketing, financing, trade development, and more. As part of the Commercial Service-State Partnership Program, the "Branding Africa" program is also increasing the Africa focus in the United States through the International Buyer Program (IBP). In order to attract more U.S. firms to Africa, the Commercial Service offices in Dakar, Johannesburg, and Nairobi have partnered with 37 non-Commercial Service embassies in Africa to recruit continent-wide delegations to U.S. trade shows that participate in the 2008 IBP. Fourteen non-Commercial Service embassies are expected to participate in the Partnership Program during 2008.

9 Ibid., 96.

Five New OPIC Funds for New Investment Support: In February 2008, President George W. Bush announced that OPIC would support five new private equity investment funds designed to invest in a variety of sectors vital to Africa's economic development, including health care, housing, telecommunications, and SMEs. The new commitments represent the largest single-day announcement in the history of the agency's investment funds program. "Last year, we launched the Africa Financial Sector Initiative. As part of this effort, OPIC mobilized $750 million in investment capital for African businesses," President Bush said in a speech on the eve of his February 15–21, 2008, trip to Benin, Tanzania, Rwanda, Ghana, and Liberia. "Today, I'm announcing that OPIC will support five new investment funds that will mobilize an additional $875 million, for a total of more than $1.6 billion in new capital."

USTDA Africa Trade Lanes Partnership: In April 2008, USTDA Director Larry W. Walther officially launched the African Trade Lanes Partnership at the African Growth and Opportunity Act (AGOA) Transportation and Trade Forum. The Partnership will support a coordinated intermodal transportation infrastructure program that enables Africa to better take advantage of the AGOA benefits. Director Walther joined a U.S. Department of Transportation delegation led by Deputy Secretary Thomas Barrett on a four-country tour of Africa to promote the strengthening of transportation linkages throughout the continent. The African Trade Lanes Partnership seeks to advance the development of sub-Saharan Africa's most vital trade lanes and transportation networks to facilitate local, regional, and global trade. The initiative is designed to promote regional cooperation and connectivity in all modes of transportation, including aviation, maritime, land, and rail. During the two-year initiative, USTDA will provide $4 million for transportation infrastructure planning across sub-Saharan Africa, including technical assistance, investment analysis, business workshops, training, project definition, and other critical trade capacity building activities. As an initial activity under the initiative, Director Walther signed an agreement awarding a $725,050 grant to the Zambian Ministry of Communications and Transport.

Commercial Service Trade Mission to Sub-Saharan Africa: In March 2008, Commercial Service Director General Israel Hernandez led 22 business professionals representing 13 U.S. firms on a strategic business tour of sub-Saharan Africa, visiting Accra, Ghana; Lagos, Nigeria; and Johannesburg, South Africa. The delegation's diversity in terms of company size, sectors, and goals offered an impressive representation of the dynamism and strength of the U.S. business community. Mission participants benefited from customized matchmaking, market briefings, networking, and counseling in each country.

Ex-Im Bank Delegated Authority for African Export-Import Bank: To make it easier and faster for African buyers to obtain Ex-Im Bank support for their purchases of U.S. goods and services, Ex-Im Bank approved special delegated authority for the African Export-Import Bank (Afreximbank) to provide up to $40 million in Ex-Im Bank short-term and medium-term financing. With this authorization, Afreximbank will have the credit capacity to finance multiple Ex-Im Bank-backed short-term and medium-term transactions with less administrative involvement by Ex-Im Bank staff and reduced processing time. The primary source of repayment will be Afreximbank. In addition, the facility will serve as a new marketing tool

for both Ex-Im Bank and Afreximbank to promote the purchase of U.S. goods and services in Africa. "This facility provides tremendous opportunity for Afreximbank to support our numerous clients in oil services, aviation, manufacturing, telecommunications, and power. The doors are now open to our clients to consider the U.S. market as they source raw materials and equipment for export manufacturing, infrastructure, and related projects," says Afreximbank President Jean-Louis Ekra.

USDA African Growth and Opportunity Act (AGOA) Initiatives: At the sixth AGOA Forum in Ghana in July 2007, Under Secretary of Agriculture Mark Keenum announced four initiatives (West and Central African trade and investment mission; Namibian beef equivalency training; scientific exchange in cocoa production; and organic certification training) to help sub-Saharan countries bolster agricultural exports to the United States. FAS Administrator Mike Yost led a trade and investment mission to Kenya in February of 2007. The mission helped to connect 15 U.S. agribusinesses with 50 African agribusiness representatives. As a result of this activity, U.S. companies achieved more than $750,000 in new sales. USDA participated in Trade and Investment Framework Agreement (TIFA) meetings in Mauritius, Rwanda, Liberia, Nigeria, and Ghana. In March 2008, FAS Associate Administrator Constance Jackson led 19 U.S. agribusiness firms on the Agribusiness Trade and Investment Mission to West and Central Africa.[10] Participant countries included Benin, Burkina Faso, Cameroon, Cape Verde, Ghana, Liberia, Mali, Nigeria, Senegal, Sierra Leone, and Togo.

State Department/Digital Freedom Initiative: The President's Digital Freedom Initiative (DFI)—a partnership among multiple Federal agencies, industry, non-profit and non-governmental organizations, and universities—aims to expand connectivity throughout the world. DFI has been engaged in several Africa-focused projects, including a roundtable dialogue with African Ministers of Communication in Washington and San Francisco in March 2007

10 www.fas.usda.gov/icd/AfricaTradeMission2008/index.asp

and a Ministerial-Level East Africa Broadband Workshop in Kigali, Rwanda in May 2007. In July 2008, DFI held a West Africa ICT Conference. In addition, DFI also co-hosted the first ever "Technology and Emerging Countries" event at the International Consumer Electronics Show, January, 2008 in Las Vegas, Nevada. Paul Kagame, President of Rwanda, was hosted as a keynote speaker.

Selected TPCC Agencies' Accomplishments in Fiscal Year (FY) 2007

U.S. DEPARTMENT OF COMMERCE

Strategy:

- Open and expand foreign markets for U.S. goods and services and improve the Nation's export performance.

- Promote U.S. export growth through implementation of the National Export Strategy by:

  Expanding and enhancing cooperation with partnership organizations so that U.S. businesses benefit from global business.

  Ensuring that U.S. businesses benefit from free trade negotiations and through identified priority markets.

  Ensuring that U.S. small and medium-sized enterprises (SMEs) and manufacturers can compete and win in the global economy.

  Fostering a level playing field for U.S. firms at home and abroad through development of trade policy positions, advancement of negotiating positions, and effective enforcement of U.S. trade laws and bilateral and multilateral agreements intended to combat foreign unfair trading practices.

- Ensure that export controls do not unduly disadvantage U.S. firms in world markets by eliminating outdated controls and streamlining the process for obtaining export licenses for products that remain under export controls.

Results:

- In 2007, the Department of Commerce continued to expand its outreach to strategic partners, including U.S. cities and States, corporate partners, and trade associations. The Commercial Service is incorporating States' course content and participants in trade specialist training programs. The Commercial Service increased the number of corporate partners from six in 2007 to 12 in 2008, including TD Commerce Bank, the U.S. Postal Service, City National Bank, Baker & McKenzie, Zions Bank, and Comerica Bank. These partners join Commercial Service's ongoing partnerships with FedEx, UPS, PNC Bank, M&T Bank, eBay, and Google. In 2007, the Commercial Service maintained active cooperation with the District Export Councils and instituted an Associations Bulletin on Commercial Service activities.

- In 2007, CAFTA-DR entered into force with the Dominican Republic. Also in 2007, the U.S. and Peruvian Congresses approved the U.S.-Peru Trade Promotion Agreement, and President Bush signed the U.S.-Peru TPA Implementation Act. In FY 2007, the Commercial Service achieved 1,773 export successes for U.S. companies exporting to the 14 countries with FTAs in force in 2007.

- In 2007, the Asia team of ITA's Market Access and Compliance (MAC) unit provided strong leadership and/or support for negotiations and policy discussions for the U.S.-Japan Regulatory Reform and Investment Initiative under the Economic Partnership for Growth, the U.S.-China Joint Commission on Commerce and Trade (JCCT), the U.S.-China Strategic Economic Dialogue, the U.S.-Korea Free Trade Agreement, the Asia-Pacific Economic Cooperation forum, and the Association of Southeast Asian Nations Enhanced Partnership with the United States.

- In 2007, the Commercial Service helped generate nearly 12,000 export successes worth billions of dollars in U.S. export sales, including firms that exported for the first time, entered a new market, or increased their market share in an existing market. During FY 2007, the Commercial Service piloted a "commercial diplomacy" success metric to measure its performance in resolving a company's problems in a market, reducing trade barriers, and cutting red tape.

- MAC has a sizable caseload from U.S. firms that have encountered trade barriers. In FY 2007, MAC initiated 187 cases from U.S. industry and resolved 158. For the past four years, ITA has met or exceeded targets for the number of cases initiated and the number of cases resolved. In 2007, ITA's trade compliance team received 180 formal inquiries from individuals or companies through the stopfakes.gov Web site, part of the STOP! (Strategy Targeting Organized Piracy) campaign.

- In 2007, ITA's Import Administration (IA) reversed its long-standing general practice of not applying the countervailing duty (CVD) law to non-market economies. Because of changes in China's economy, IA began to apply the CVD law to China, even while it remained a non-market economy under U.S. unfair trade laws. This precedent-setting decision permits many U.S. industries that had long complained about the harm caused by subsidized imports from China to seek relief under the CVD law. This change thus significantly adds to the range of tools available to the Department of Commerce to address unfair trade from that country. Since this decision, IA has found imports from China to be subsidized in seven separate investigations and is examining alleged subsidies in five additional ongoing investigations, covering imports from China totaling more than $1.2 billion.

- In 2007, IA conducted more than 100 pre-petition counseling sessions with SMEs to explain the remedies available under U.S. antidumping and CVD laws, help determine whether these laws could address their particular trade concern, and provide guidance and assistance in preparing a petition.

- As part of its effort to open large, fast-growing emerging markets, the Department of Commerce has led several important trade events during the past year. The June 2007 Americas Competitiveness Forum in Atlanta, Georgia, drew approximately 1,000 business and government representatives from throughout the Western Hemisphere. In 2007, Secretary of Commerce Carlos M. Gutierrez led a trade mission of American companies to Vietnam, launched the first U.S.-Brazil CEO Forum with counterparts in Brazil, and traveled to India to expand the bilateral economic relationship. ITA Assistant Secretary David Bohigian led Clean Energy Trade Missions to China and India in January 2008. In April 2008, ITA Under Secretary Christopher A. Padilla led a Health Care Policy Mission to China. These trade events provide U.S. companies better access to these often challenging markets.

- The Department of Commerce's Bureau of Industry and Security (BIS) processed 19,512 export license applications and related requests in FY 2007. While this represented an increase over the amount processed in FY 2006, the Department continued to process these applications in a timely manner. As part of its mission to keep U.S. firms informed of export control regulations, BIS launched the BIS Online Training Room offering an introductory series of modules covering materials from the Essentials of Export Controls seminars currently offered around the country. This free service is intended to save exporters—particularly SMEs—time and money.

EXPORT-IMPORT BANK OF THE UNITED STATES

Strategy:

- Attending to the needs of small business exporters. Building on the creation in 2006 of the Small Business Division to further Ex-Im Bank's outreach and business development efforts, the Bank established designated specialists throughout its operating units who devote their attention and expertise to the processing of small-business transactions.

- Making it easier for our customers to do business with the Bank. Ex-Im Online, the Bank's Web-based application and transaction-management system, has been operational for two years. Ex-Im Bank will continue to enhance and improve this system to maximize efficiency and to reduce paperwork and processing times while increasing the transparency of our operations.

- Adapting to meet the needs of a dynamic global marketplace. Some export credit agencies are taking on the characteristics of the private sector, while others in emerging markets are growing rapidly, unconstrained by the export credit guidelines of the Organization for Economic Cooperation and Development (OECD). To keep pace with the changing marketplace, Ex-Im Bank will deepen existing relationships with OECD member export credit agencies and build new relationships with rising export credit agencies.

- Expanding the partner network of financial institutions, export credit insurance brokers, city/State partners, and industry associations.

- Increasing its financing support for sales of U.S. goods and services to countries in sub-Saharan Africa.

Results:

- In FY 2007, Ex-Im Bank provided more than $12.5 billion in new authorizations to more than 65 countries.

- Ex-Im Bank authorized $3.4 billion in small-business transactions, accounting for 26 percent of total authorizations and 85 percent of total transactions. As of January 2007, Ex-Im Bank transitioned all short-term transaction processing and almost all medium-term guarantee transaction processing (excluding working capital) onto Ex-Im Online. A recent analysis indicated that the majority of these short- and medium-term applications and shipment reports are being directly submitted to Ex-Im Bank through the online system.

- Ex-Im Bank has established a working relationship with the Export-Import Bank of China. As a result, these two export credit agencies have created a framework agreement to facilitate the financing of U.S. exports of medium-term goods and services to China. Under this framework, Ex-Im Bank has supported four transactions in FY 2007 and FY 2008 to date, totaling more than $207 million, with an additional three possible applications in the pipeline. Discussions are ongoing regarding other areas of cooperation.

- In FY 2007, Ex-Im Bank authorized $1.3 billion in working capital, with 77 percent of these authorizations supporting small business exporters.

- In FY 2007, Ex-Im Bank authorized more than $430 million in support of U.S. exports to 18 different markets in sub-Saharan Africa.

OVERSEAS PRIVATE INVESTMENT CORPORATION

Strategy:

- By focusing on housing and access to credit, OPIC is developing dynamic catalysts for private-sector-led growth in the development of "entrepreneurial capitalism" as a soft power tool of U.S. foreign policy.

- By reaching out in more ways to U.S. small businesses as well as minority- and woman-owned enterprises, OPIC ensures greater access to opportunity for more U.S. businesses.

- By charging market-based fees for its products, OPIC continues to meet these responsibilities as a self-sustaining agency, operating at no net cost to taxpayers and returning money to the U.S. Treasury.

Results:

- In the West Bank, OPIC announced a $228 million small business lending facility. Working with local financial institutions, the facility is providing loans to Palestinian small businesses, thus helping small businesses grow and providing employment and economic growth.

- In Jordan, OPIC approved a $70 million power project, as well as $220 million of potential investment, through three investment funds focused on Jordan for small business development, housing, water, and energy.

- In Latin America, OPIC collectively supported $870 million in mobilized capital in four projects and two investment funds that focus on mortgage markets and construction loans throughout Latin America, with a focus on Central America. OPIC also hosted its annual investment conference in San Salvador, El Salvador.

- In sub-Saharan Africa, OPIC has worked with private investors to support creation of the $30 million Liberian Enterprise Development Fund to support private-sector-led economic development in Liberia. In addition, OPIC announced three new investment funds focused on sub-Saharan Africa that will mobilize $750 million to support African capital markets.

- To extend and augment its commitment to U.S. small business, OPIC launched the $100 million Enterprise Development Network (EDN) designed to target U.S. small business projects in developing countries by leveraging U.S. banks' extensive grassroots networks across the country and their unique knowledge of markets. Working with financial institutions, OPIC has improved access to credit for SMEs and microfinance entities to promote effective development.

- OPIC concluded a seven-city series of workshops across the country focused on informing woman-owned and minority-owned businesses of the services and programs that OPIC can offer in making their businesses grow internationally.

- In FY 2007, OPIC returned $192 million to the U.S. Treasury after deducting for its operating costs.

U.S. TRADE AND DEVELOPMENT AGENCY

Strategy:

- Continue to target programs that open markets for U.S. industry while supporting economic development in foreign markets.

- Focus attention on building the infrastructure for development; supporting U.S. trade policy; enhancing regional integration initiatives; enhancing global energy security; and strengthening transportation safety and security.

- Expand the agency's outreach to the U.S. business community with a particular focus on SMEs that may be able to take advantage of USTDA's programs while increasing their international exposure.

Results:

- USTDA further implemented its CAFTA-DR Trade Integration Initiative through targeted infrastructure and trade facilitation support that leverages existing U.S. Government development assistance programs in El Salvador.

- Over the last 10-year period, USTDA has identified more than $39 in U.S. exports associated with every dollar invested by USTDA in projects around the world.

- USTDA expanded its outreach to U.S. industry through an increase in site visits and participation in business briefings with foreign delegates who traveled to the United States to see the world's best manufacturing base.

U.S. SMALL BUSINESS ADMINISTRATION

Strategy:

- Structure and service delivery improvements resulting in record loan numbers to small businesses.

- SME Congress of the Americas: SBA's noted support of the Summit of the Americas Process.

- SBA/Ex-Im Bank co-guarantee: "thinking outside the box" and being a good U.S. Government partner.

Results:

- SBA made 2,968 export loans in FY 2007 for more than $800 million. These loans generated nearly $2 billion in export sales. SBA's U.S. Export Assistance Center (USEAC) representatives also provided counseling and training to more than 10,000 small businesses.

- The SME Congress of the Americas is a hemispheric network promoting and facilitating the participation of small business in trade. SBA spearheaded and leads this initiative. In 2007, SBA worked closely with Mexican counterparts to compose an inter-institutional MOU on the SME Congress of the Americas on international trade to formalize the steering committee and institutionalize agency commitment to advancing this Summit of the Americas deliverable. In 2007, the SME Congress, under SBA's leadership, conducted a multi-national videoconference on "Bridging the Americas through Small Business Trade." Participating sites included Washington, D.C.; Florida; Mexico; Puerto Rico; Chile; Costa Rica; and the Dominican Republic. This videoconference was a precursor to a multi-sector International Small Business Networking event held during the annual conference of the U.S. Hispanic Chamber of Commerce in Puerto Rico. Approximately 50 companies from seven countries participated and provided very positive feedback. SBA continues to work closely with the Departments of State and Commerce to support and advance the Summit of the Americas Process through the SME Congress initiative.

- SBA's Office of International Trade (OIT) continues to work with Ex-Im Bank to implement a joint-marketing plan and to harmonize SBA's and Ex-Im Bank's export working capital programs. The marketing plan was created to enhance service and delivery through outreach and collaboration to U.S. banks, as well as to provide joint marketing information on each agency's programs and products for small business exporters, and make joint business calls when able. USEAC staff has made more than 40 EWCP loans under this collaboration. OIT also finalized its strategy and outreach plan to recruit and/or provide SBA EWCP-Preferred Lender Program (PLP) status to existing as well as new participating lenders in trade finance. SBA's OIT also represented SBA at the Ex-Im Bank training Conference.

U.S. DEPARTMENT OF AGRICULTURE, FOREIGN AGRICULTURAL SERVICE

Strategy:

- Expand and maintain international export opportunities.

- Support international economic development and trade capacity building.

- Improve sanitary and phytosanitary (SPS) systems to facilitate agricultural trade.

Results:

- In FY 2007, USDA activities included completing new free trade agreements, opening new international markets, and maintaining existing markets. To expand overseas markets and facilitate trade, USDA assists in the negotiation, monitoring, and enforcement of trade agreements. Working with producers and commodity trade associations, USDA administers an array of market development and export promotion programs designed to build long-term markets abroad. The Department helps expand trade opportunities through technical assistance and training programs and works to facilitate trade by adopting science-based regulatory systems and standards. USDA staff in more than 80 countries help to open, retain, and expand international markets for U.S. food and agricultural products.

- U.S. agricultural exports rose to a record $81.9 billion in FY 2007, up $13.3 billion from the previous year. Canada remains our largest export market at a record $13.2 billion in FY 2007, Mexico is second at $12.3 billion, Japan is third at $9.6 billion, the EU-27 is fourth at $8 billion, and China is fifth, with export sales of $7 billion.

- USDA works closely with USTR and other U.S. Government agencies to pursue new trade agreements; to enforce the provisions of existing agreements; and to maintain effective government-to-government relationships that support open trade, leading to increased export opportunities for U.S. farmers and agribusinesses. USDA's industry partners promote trade and outreach activities to educate producers, processors, and exporters on market opportunities that result from trade agreements. To capitalize on trade opportunities, USDA offers market intelligence, supply and demand forecasts, and sales-development assistance to enhance U.S. exporters' success in the highly competitive global marketplace.

- USDA increased access to the global market by preserving trade opportunities through monitoring and compliance enforcement, overseas advocacy, and negotiations of technical protocols. The FAS Office of Country and Regional Affairs was created to develop and oversee country, regional, and cross-cutting strategies. FAS also developed a tracking system to monitor foreign trading partners' compliance with U.S. bilateral, regional, and multilateral trade agreements with regard to agricultural products. The dollar value of agricultural trade preserved through trade agreement negotiation, monitoring and enforcement (non-SPS) totaled $670 million in FY 2007.

- The United States is the world's leader in food aid, providing more than half of total worldwide assistance to combat malnutrition. U.S. food aid programs are a joint effort across several Federal departments. USDA works with the USAID, and other Federal agencies, private voluntary relief and development organizations, U.S. universities, and the World Food Program to provide targeted food aid and assistance. During the past two decades, the Food for Progress Program has supplied more than 12 million metric tons of commodities to developing countries and emerging democracies committed to introducing and expanding free enterprise in the agricultural sector. In addition, the McGovern-Dole International Food for Education and Child Nutrition Program provides for the donation of U.S. agricultural commodities and associated financial and technical assistance to carry out pre-school and school feeding programs in foreign countries. In the last five years, the McGovern-Dole Program has helped feed more than 10 million children in over 40 countries. These activities, combined with USDA technical assistance and training, foster stable societies, economic growth, and market-infrastructure development. In FY 2007, substantive improvement was made in 13 countries in the areas of national trade policy and regulatory frameworks to increase market access.

- USDA fostered an improved global SPS system for facilitating agricultural trade by addressing SPS measures and other Technical Barriers to Trade (TBT), and by monitoring international regulatory activities. USDA agencies work with other Federal agencies to address and mitigate SPS measures imposed by foreign governments. USDA leads federal efforts to monitor adherence to the SPS Agreement of the WTO, and helps lead enforcement of the agreement. Additionally, USDA conducts regulatory capacity-building activities with select trading partners. In FY 2007, USDA preserved $2.5 billion in trade through staff interventions leading to resolution of barriers created by SPS or TBT measures.

U.S. DEPARTMENT OF STATE

Strategy:

- Promote international support for a "total economic engagement" approach to poverty reduction, food security, and sustainable economic growth, by leading cooperative efforts with multilateral financial and assistance organizations, the MCC, and other U.S. aid agencies. Support international financial institutions' efforts to encourage pro-market economic reforms and financial sector development.

- Advance the Doha Round and bilateral efforts to conclude FTAs by supporting U.S. Government efforts, including protection and enforcement of U.S. intellectual property rights overseas and reduction of trade barriers for agricultural exports.

- Develop international communications policies that are vital for our economic and military security; trade in goods and services; e-commerce; intellectual property protection; and the fostering of democratic societies. Ensure market access, freedom of technology choice, the integrity of the Internet, and adherence to international standards by leading multilateral and bilateral efforts to devise and implement initiatives in these areas.

- Promote transparent and open energy investment regimes and markets, strategic petroleum stockholding, diverse and secure energy supplies and sources, and development of clean alternative energy technologies that are vital to long-term U.S. energy security.

- Negotiate air services agreements, seeking to foster competition among airlines by removing restrictions on the number of carriers, routes, aircraft, services, and prices.

- Improve business and investment climates abroad through the negotiation of bilateral investment treaties (State-USTR co-lead), investment, and IPR chapters of free trade agreements (USTR lead), and ongoing policy dialogues.

- Advocate for U.S. companies to ensure fair play, assist with regulatory and investment problems (including intellectual property protection and enforcement), and maximize commercial opportunities

- Improve support for U.S. business overseas, particularly at those 100 embassies that do not have a Commercial Service office ("non-Commercial Service"), at which State's economic officers are responsible for providing commercial services.

- Organize conferences to promote trade and investment in strategic countries and regions.

- Build the capacity of foreign police, prosecutors, border and customs officials, and judges in the fight against IP crime by funding law enforcement training and technical assistance.

Results:

- The Department of State provided advocacy services for 335 company-specific cases and recorded 60 success stories during 2007. An increased emphasis on tracking commercial advocacy supports our outreach efforts to Congressional offices, to the U.S. business community, and to foreign governments.

- The State Department hosted 132 business outreach programs during 2007, promoting best business practices, public diplomacy goals, and awareness and understanding of U.S. Government policy affecting U.S. business abroad.

- The Department of State signed an MOU with the Commercial Service on April 20, 2008, to formalize the Joint Commercial Service-State Post Partnership Program. The formal relationship will support regional partnership programs established between 100 non-Commercial Service embassies and nearby Commercial Service offices. During 2007, the State Department funded trade fairs, trade capacity-building seminars, and business outreach activities in more than 65 non-Commercial Service embassies to further support commercial diplomacy efforts in the host country.

- Fifty-eight IPR training and technical assistance projects, totaling $11.9 million over the past five years, have been funded by the Bureau of International Narcotics and Law Enforcement Affairs and the Bureau of Economic and Business Affairs.

TPCC PROGRAM BUDGET AUTHORITY, IN MILLIONS OF DOLLARS

	FY 2007 Actual	FY 2008 Enacted	FY 2009 Request
Department of Agriculture	674	644	563
Department of Commerce	356	339	350
Department of State[1]	176	184	198
Department of the Treasury	3	3	3
Export-Import Bank	38	1	3
Overseas Private Investment Corporation[2]	(192)	(165)	(170)
Small Business Administration	5.2	6	6.4
U.S. Trade and Development Agency	50	51	51
U.S. Trade Representative	44	44	46
Total	**1,346**	**1,272**	**1,220**

Note:

Amounts may be restated in the future to reflect new data or definitions. Figures may include administrative expenses, transfers, or other adjustments.

[1]Dollars are cumulative of all business and economic activities in the State Department.

[2]Totals do not include OPIC.

Status of 2007 National Export Strategy Recommendations

The table below tracks the implementation of priority initiatives highlighted in the prior year's annual report. Page numbers in the left column refer to the 2007 National Export Strategy, a full version of which can be viewed or downloaded at www.ita. doc.gov/media/Publications/pdf/nes2007FINAL.pdf. Page numbers in the right column refer to this report—the 2008 National Export Strategy.

STATE OF TRADE

Department of Commerce (DOC) — Transformational Commercial Diplomacy (p. 20)	Update: The Commercial Service (CS) has closed 22 offices. Four offices have opened (Qatar, Tunisia, Libya, and Afghanistan). Additional offices in Brazil, China, India, and Azerbaijan are planned for 2009.
DOC — Invest in America (p. 21)	See p. 11, State of Trade — Inaugural "Invest in America" Week in 18 states.
DOC — Services Sector Promotion	Update: In 2007 and 2008, using a $3.9 million appropriation, the Department of Commerce implemented a third round of television and underground advertising utilizing the original creative, "You've Seen the Films, Now Visit the Set." The Visit USA UK Association reported a 6.6 percent increase in unique site visits, and a nearly 200 percent increase in brochure requests as a result of the campaign, the only metrics available for this last round of the campaign.
U.S. Tourism Promotion Campaign and $3.9 million Advisory Board/Travel Industry Association (TIA) Website (p. 22)	Update: The Department of Commerce awarded a cooperative agreement to the Travel Industry Association (TIA) for the development of a consumer Web site to market the United States as a destination in the five largest international traveler source markets (Canada, Germany, Japan, Mexico, and the United Kingdom). In April 2008, TIA launched the Web site DiscoverAmerica.com. More than 15,000 pages of information about the destinations, products and services of the U.S. travel product are available through the site, which has also been translated into French, German, Japanese, and Spanish. TIA continues to add content and is working closely with a subcontractor to develop strategic partnerships that will sustain the site after the monies from the cooperative agreement have been exhausted.
Franchising — landmark CS-International Franchise Association agreement (p. 23)	Update: Initiatives such as a Franchise Knowledge Education Program and increased high profile participation at the International Franchise Association (IFA) Convention have greatly helped to advance mutual interests in helping the U.S. franchising community expand in international markets. The benefits of this enhanced partnership are most evident in terms of the number of CS export successes reported by clients in 2007, which increased by 130 percent from 2006. Joint 2007 CS/IFA activities resulting from the agreement include: Mexico Franchise Fair, India Franchise Show, Middle East Franchise Show (Dubai), Paris Franchise Show, American Franchise Forum (Panama), Ireland/UK Franchising Seminar, Franchise Development Conference (Cairo), and Franchising and Licensing Asia (Singapore).

Education — Electronic Education Fair Initiative — China pilot and expansion to India (p. 24)	Update: In 2007, ChinaTV pilot programming reached 180 million people and the China landing page (www.liuxueasa.cn) had more than 600,000 visits, about 97 percent from within China. In December 2007, the Department of Commerce broadcast documentaries in India. Indian students were interviewed and filmed at 17 different U.S. institutions of higher education. The India programs are available at www.NamasteStudyUSA.com.
State — Facilitating business travel to the U.S. (p. 25)	Update: The State Department continues to update visa reciprocity agreements with many nations. U.S. officials are working closely with American Chambers of Commerce in more than 100 countries to expedite the visa process for legitimate business travelers. State's Business Visa Center in Washington, D.C., handled more than 5,000 requests from American businesses in cases involving more than 311,000 business travelers in FY 2007. The Bureau of Consular Affairs has made changes that enhance the efficiency, predictability, and transparency of the visa process, including establishment of an Internet-based visa appointment system.

IMPACT OF TRADE LIBERALIZATION

CAFTA-DR

OPIC — Access to Opportunity Conference (p. 40)	See p. 46, Free Trade Agreements — OPIC event resulted in 300 participants from 15 countries.
USTDA — CAFTA-DR Trade Integration Initiative (p. 40)	See p. 46-47, Free Trade Agreements — USTDA expands Initiative to El Salvador, Costa Rica, and Guatemala.
USDA — recognition of U.S. food safety inspection (p. 41)	See p. 45, Free Trade Agreements — USDA market access approach. Note: increase in U.S. agricultural exports to CAFTA-DR from $2.2 billion in 2006 to $2.8 billion in 2007.
DOC — TPCC agency support/outreach (p. 42)	See p. 45, Free Trade Agreements — Commercial Service Trade Americas FTA Roadshow during World Trade Month in May 2008.
SBA — SME Congress of the Americas (p. 42)	See p. 53, Priority Markets — SBA activities at the Third SME Congress, including Steering Committee and SME panel.

Middle East Free Trade Area Initiative (MEFTA)

USTDA — Jordan, Morocco initiatives (p. 42)	See p. 47, Free Trade Agreements — Wastewater and solid waste treatment projects in Jordan and Morocco.
OPIC — New Jordan funds (p. 43)	See p. 70, Next Generation Markets — The OPIC May 2008 Access to Opportunities in the Middle East Conference incorporated sessions featuring OPIC fund managers, including SME financing, access to capital, and housing.
Ex-Im Bank — Morocco MOU (p. 43)	Update: Ex-Im Bank co-hosted a day-long seminar June 17, 2008, in Casablanca, Morocco.
DOC — planned business conference in Jordan (p. 44)	See p. 69, Next Generation Markets — Results of February 2008 U.S.-Middle East and North Africa Trade and Investment Conference in Jordan.
State — MEFTA Conference (p. 44)	Completed.
FAS — workshops in Yemen, Bahrain, UAE (p. 44)	Completed.

Other FTAs

Ex-Im Bank – Boeing aircraft sales to Australia, Chile, Singapore (p. 45)	Completed.
USTDA – Chile environmental cooperation (p. 45)	Update: In September 2007, USTDA hosted a weeklong visit by a 12-person Chilean delegation from the government and the private sector to tour U.S. geothermal companies, institutions, and plants, and to attend the annual meeting of the Geothermal Resources Council in Reno, Nevada.

RISE OF E-COMMERCE

DOC — Featured U.S. Exporters (FUSE) program (p. 70)	See p. 34, Broadening and Deepening the Base of Exporters – Expansion of FUSE to 60 markets.
Ex-Im Bank — Ex-Im Online (p.71)	See p. 35, Broadening and Deepening the Base of Exporters – Additional services now available on-line.
State — Digital Freedom Initiative (DFI) (p. 71)	See p. 73, Next Generation Markets — Recent and planned DFI events in Africa.
DOC — Improved Selling Online services (p. 72)	Update: In 2008, the Department of Commerce's first new edition of A Basic Guide to Exporting since 1998 will include a new chapter on "Going Online: E-Exporting Tools for Small Businesses." This chapter includes advice on types of e-commerce Web sites, conducting IT assessments, steps to going online, executing orders, and providing after-sales service, in addition to key legal and regulatory considerations in the global marketplace. A Basic Guide to Exporting will be distributed through various partners and will be available through the Government Printing Office's online bookstore.
DOC — Promotion of Web Applications for Business (p. 73)	See p. 26, Broadening and Deepening — Web Revolution seminar series with corporate partners Google, FedEx, and Baker & McKenzie.

STRATEGIC PARTNERSHIPS

States

FAS — NCSL dialogue and SRTG outreach (p. 84)	See p. 23, 24 Broadening and Deepening — Update on NCSL and SRTG activities.
DOC — professional development, outreach, information sharing, relationship management (p. 85)	Update: CS has worked with the State International Development Organization (SIDO) to address coordination of trade promotion activities and sharing of credit for export assistance efforts. CS plans to provide information from its new Client Tracking System that does not contain proprietary information to State trade agencies, and will look at additional ways to share information. CS will continue to collocate with State trade agencies when practical. CS also regularly includes State trade representatives in the TPCC Interagency Trade Officer Training Program and has begun getting state trade agencies involved in ITA's industry and regional teams. To strengthen the partnership with the States, SIDO members have been added to the CS marketing database so they receive timely notice of upcoming trade events. Also, SIDO members now have a formal channel through CS domestic networks to provide feedback on the effectiveness of local U.S. Export Assistance Centers and their relationships with States that will be considered when evaluating trade specialist performance.
Ex-Im Bank — City/State Partners Program (p. 88)	See p. 24, Broadening and Deepening — Expansion to nine new partners.

OPIC — Women & Minority-Owned Workshops (p. 88)	See p. 35, Broadening and Deepening — New series launched in September 2007.
USTDA — Outreach to States (p. 89)	Update: In May 2007, USTDA and other agencies participated in the "Governor's Global Trade Conference" in Minnesota with more than 100 participants. In June 2007, USTDA and Ex-Im Bank partnered with Maryland, Virginia, and Washington, D.C., for a conference focused on information technology, transportation infrastructure, agribusiness, and environment with 150 participants.

Associations

FAS — MAP, USEADC, Trade Shows and Cochran Fellowship Program (p. 91)	See p. 30, Broadening and Deepening — MAP, trade show, and USEADC activity. Supplemental data:
	MAP: Performance data reported through the Program Assessment Rating Tool in November of 2007 include: 1) an increase in exports to targeted markets of $6 billion from 2005 to 2006 largely attributable to the MAP; 2) actual sales for small companies of $459 million; and 3) the Export Multiplier Ratio (measure of total exports to targeted markets divided by costs) increased by 6.4 from 2005 to 2006. A cost-benefit analysis of MAP in 2006 confirmed that industry, not government, provides the majority of funding to carry out overseas market development activities.
	Cochran Fellowship Program: Provided short-term training in the U.S. for 706 international participants from 70 countries in FY 2007. Since its inception in 1984, the Program has provided training to almost 13,000 participants from over 100 countries.
DOC — Planned outreach and joint projects, including DEC (p. 93)	See p. 32, 33, Broadening and Deepening — Update on National DEC Conference, Export University, and New Association Bulletin.
State — BCIU training initiatives (p. 94)	See p 31, 32, Broadening and Deepening — Update on BCIU-organized Ambassadors' consultations, Commercial Diplomacy Training, TPCC Interagency Training, and Corporate Practicum program.
Ex-Im Bank — Packaging Machinery Manufacturers Institute (p. 95)	Ongoing partnership.

Corporate Partners

DOC — corporate partners program (p. 96)	See p. 24-27, Broadening and Deepening — expansion of CS' corporate partners program to new partners and ongoing development of metrics.
OPIC — Enterprise Development Network (p. 103)	See p. 26-28, Broadening and Deepening — Official June 2007 launch and selection of EDN partners.
SBA — trade-related support of resource partners (p. 104)	See p. 29, Broadening and Deepening — SBA and ASBDC inaugural Small Business International Trade Symposium in Hialeah, Florida, with support of CS, city, State, DEC, and corporate partners. TPCC International Trade Certificate Course at the ASBDC Annual Conference, September 2008 in Chicago, Illinois.
State — Economic Empowerment in Strategic Regions Initiative (p. 104)	Update: Economic Empowerment in Strategic Regions (EESR) is an interagency initiative led by the U.S. State Department which seeks to harness the power of the U.S. private sector in the fight against extremism around the globe. The goal of EESR is to promote sustainable private-sector job creation as an alternative to extremism. The program uses a Web-based platform to solicit business proposals from small to medium-sized entrepreneurs in targeted areas. Proposals are then reviewed by volunteer MBA students in the United States, and posted to the EESR Web site and marketed to potential partners and funding sources. EESR is a mechanism through which U.S. companies can be linked with individual opportunities for investment, strategic partnerships or joint ventures. The first pilot region is the Afghanistan/Pakistan border area, and business proposals have already been received and are under review. More information can be found at the EESR Web site at www.state.gov/e/eeb/tpp/eesr/.

China

IPR (p. 108-109)	See p. 56, Priority Markets — JCCT cooperation, technical assistance conference, China IPR Advisory Program, and China IPR Webinar series.
Trade Promotion Infrastructure (p. 109-111)	See p. 57, Priority Markets — CS Trade Promotion Calendar: U.S. Pavilions at Chinese trade shows.
	Update: In February 2008, Ex-Im Bank supported the first transaction under its framework agreement with China's Ministry of Finance, signed in 2005. Chindex International Inc. in Bethesda, MD will export U.S. medical equipment with the support of a seven-year $4.5 million loan guarantee from Ex-Im Bank.
	Update: The ACP is a public-private partnership of the USTDA, the U.S. Federal Aviation Administration, the Civil Aviation Administration of China (CAAC), and the U.S. aviation industry to engage the CAAC through training on priority development projects. Most recently, a $1.7 million USTDA grant was awarded in July 2007 to support this technical cooperation initiative.
	Update: U.S. food and agriculture exports to China have risen dramatically over the past five years, reaching $8.8 billion in 2006 and $10.7 billion in 2007. In May 2007, USDA promoted the SIAL China 2007 trade show. Forty-four companies participated, introducing over 300 new products with on-site sales of $900,000 and 12-month projected sales of nearly $40 million.
Focus on Second-Tier Cities and Key Sectors: Clean Energy Missions Health Care, states events, FAS market access support (p. 111-112)	Update: In 2007, American Trading Centers (ATC) generated 22 export successes, up 48 percent from 2006. ATCs also account for 28 percent of CS activity in China. (Note: In addition to the U.S. Embassy and consulates, CS offers its services through 14 American Trading Centers in second-tier cities).
	See p. 52, 53, 55, Priority Markets – Key sectors: China Health Care Trade Mission, China/India Clean Energy Trade Mission;
	See p. 55, 57, Priority Markets – FAS market access support: U.S.-China Biofuels Agreement, agricultural market access efforts, sanitary/phytosanitary technical cooperation.

India

Bilateral Dialogue (p. 114-117)	See p.59-61, Priority Markets — U.S.-India Energy Dialogue; Agricultural Knowledge Initiative and Trade Policy Forum Focus Group on Agriculture.
Business Development Mission (p. 117)	Completed.
Key sectors: Aviation Cooperation Program (ACP); U.S. suppliers to supply chain (p. 118)	See p. 60-61, Priority Markets — India Air Traffic Management Training Program in support of ACP.
	Update: Supply chain initiative suspended per the U.S. company's decision not to pursue.

Brazil

Bilateral Dialogue: (p. 120)	See p. 63-64, Priority Markets — Update of U.S.-Brazil Commercial Dialogue and U.S.-Brazil CEO Forum.
Promotion opportunities (p. 121)	See p. 64, Priority Markets — USTDA intelligent transportation system support.
	Update: Trade missions were conducted in the aerospace, energy, and healthcare sectors.

Acronyms

ACE	architecture, construction, and engineering
ACF	Americas Competitiveness Forum
ACP	Aviation Cooperation Program (U.S. Trade and Development Agency)
ACORE	American Council on Renewable Energy
AGOA	African Growth and Opportunity Act
APP	Asia Pacific Partnership on Clean Development and Climate
ASBDC	Association of Small Business Development Centers
ATMTP	Air Traffic Management Training Program (in India)
ATC	American Trading Centers (in China)
B2C	business-to-consumer
BCIU	Business Council for International Understanding
BEA	Bureau of Economic Analysis (U.S. Department of Commerce)
BIS	Bureau of Industry and Security (U.S. Department of Commerce)
BITDC	Brooklyn International Trade Development Center
BITs	bilateral investment treaties
BPE2	Second U.S.-China ACE Services Best Practices Exchange
BRIC	Brazil, Russia, India and China—"BRIC Countries"
BTI	Border Training Initiative
CAAC	Civil Aviation Administration of China
CAFTA-DR	Dominican Republic-Central America-United States Free Trade Agreement
CASS	Chinese Academy of Social Sciences
CEA ERP	Council of Economic Advisers' Economic Report of the President
CEO	Chief Executive Officer
CIFAL-Atlanta	City of Atlanta and the International Training Center for Government Authorities
CS	Commercial Service (U.S. Department of Commerce)
CVD	countervailing duty
DEC	District Export Council
DDA	Doha Development Agenda (Doha Round)
DFI	The President's Digital Freedom Initiative
ECA	export credit agency
EDN	Enterprise Development Network (OPIC)
EESR	Economic Empowerment in Strategic Regions
Ex-Im Bank	Export-Import Bank of the United States
EU	European Union
EWCP	Export Working Capital Program

FAS	Foreign Agricultural Service (U.S. Department of Agriculture)
FCC	Federal Communications Commission
FCIB	Finance, Credit, and International Business
FDI	foreign direct investment
FTA	free trade agreement
FUSE	Featured U. S. Exporter Service
FY	fiscal year
G7	Group of Seven
GCI	Global Competitiveness Index
GDeD	Georgia Department of Economic Development
GDP	Gross Domestic Product
IA	Import Administration (U.S. Department of Commerce)
IBC	India Business Center
IBP	International Buyer Program
ICT	information and communications technology
IEDC	Indiana Economic Development Corporation
IFA	International Franchise Association
IMF	International Monetary Fund
IP	intellectual property
IPR	intellectual property rights
IT	information technology
ITA	International Trade Administration
JCCT	Joint Commission on Commerce and Trade (U.S.-China)
KORUS-FTA	United States-Korea Free Trade Agreement
LAEDC	Los Angeles County Economic Development Corporation
LAGCOE	Louisiana Gulf Coast Oil Exposition
LED	Louisiana Economic Department
MAC	Market Access and Compliance (U.S. Department of Commerce)
MAP	Market Access Program
MDCP	Market Development Cooperator Program
MENA	Middle East and North Africa
MMS	Minerals Management Service (U.S. Department of the Interior)
MOC	Ministry of Construction (Russia)
MOU	memorandum of understanding
MSMEs	micro, small, and medium-sized enterprises
NAFTA	North American Free Trade Agreement
NAICS	North American Industry Classification System
NASDA	National Association of State Departments of Agriculture
NCSL	National Conference of State Legislators
NDRC	National Development and Reform Commission of China
NDTO	North Dakota Trade Office
NTIA	National Telecommunications and Information Administration
OECD	Organization for Economic Cooperation and Development
OPIC	Overseas Private Investment Corporation
PEC	President's Export Council

PLP	Preferred Lender Program
SBA	Small Business Administration
SBDC	Small Business Development Center
SCITC	South Carolina International Trade Coalition
SIDO	State International Development Organizations
SITC	Standard International Trade Classification
SMEs	small and medium-sized enterprises
SPS	sanitary/phytosanitary
SRTGs	State Regional Trade Groups
TIA	Travel Industry Association
TIFA	Trade and Investment Framework Agreement
TPA	Trade Promotion Agreement (U.S.-Peru TPA, U.S.-Panama TPA)
TPCC	Trade Promotion Coordinating Committee
TPF	U.S.-India Trade Policy Forum
TSAP	Trade Show Assistance Program
UNCTAD	United Nations Conference on Trade and Development
USAID	U.S. Agency for International Development
USDA	U.S. Department of Agriculture
USAEDC	U.S. Agricultural Export Development Council
USEACs	U.S. Export Assistance Centers
USTDA	U.S. Trade and Development Agency
USTR	Office of the United States Trade Representative
VEU	Validated End-User Program
WEF	World Economic Forum
WIREC	Washington International Renewable Energy Conference
WTO	World Trade Organization

TRADE PROMOTION

COORDINATING COMMITTEE

MEMBER AGENCIES

U.S. Department of Commerce

Export-Import Bank of the United States

Overseas Private Investment Corporation

U.S. Trade and Development Agency

U.S. Small Business Administration

U.S. Department of Agriculture

U.S. Department of State

U.S. Department of the Treasury

Office of the United States Trade Representative

U.S. Agency for International Development

U.S. Environmental Protection Agency

U.S. Department of Defense

U.S. Department of Energy

U.S. Department of Homeland Security

U.S. Department of Interior

U.S. Department of Labor

U.S. Department of Transportation

Office of Management and Budget

National Security Council/National Economic Council

Council of Economic Advisers

www.ingramcontent.com/pod-product-compliance
Lightning Source LLC
Chambersburg PA
CBHW080421290526
45791CB00008BA/2372